NEW SOIETY?

Are Social a menting?

The Editors

John Curtice is Professor of Politics at the University of Strathclyde and Research Director of the National Centre for Social Research (Scotland).

David McCrone is Professor of Sociology and co-Director of the Institute of Governance, both at the University of Edinburgh

Alison Park is a Director of the National Centre for Social Research.

Lindsay Paterson is Professor of Educational Policy at the University of Edinburgh.

The Contributors

Anne Barlow is a Senior Lecturer in Law at the University of Wales, Aberystwyth.

Catherine Bromley is a Researcher at the National Centre for Social Research (Scotland).

Kerstin Hinds is a Senior Researcher at the National Centre for Social Research (Scotland).

Lynn Jamieson is a Reader in Sociology and a co-director of the Scottish Centre for Research on Families and Relationships, both at the University of Edinburgh.

Paula Surridge is a Lecturer in Sociology at the University of Salford.

NEW SCOTLAND, NEW SOCIETY?

Are Social and Political Ties Fragmenting?

edited by

**John Curtice, David McCrone,
Alison Park and Lindsay Paterson**

POLYGON
AT EDINBURGH

Editorial arrangement © John Curtice, David McCrone,
Alison Park and Lindsay Paterson, 2002
Other material © the Contributors, 2002

Polygon at Edinburgh
An imprint of Edinburgh University Press Ltd
22 George Square, Edinburgh

Printed and bound in Great Britain by
Creative Print and Design, Ebbw Vale, Wales

A CIP Record for this book is available from the British Library

ISBN 1 902930 35 5 (paperback)

The right of the contributors to be identified as authors of this work
has been asserted in accordance with the Copyright, Designs and
Patents Act 1988.

CONTENTS

1

INTRODUCTION

This book is about what keeps Scotland together and what keeps it linked to the rest of the United Kingdom – the internal and external social ties that define the identity and boundaries of the nation. We look at them through the eyes of people in Scotland themselves – the views held by the respondents to the 2000 Scottish Social Attitudes Survey.

Scotland's external ties have been thoroughly debated over the last few years, because many people have hoped or feared that they are being attenuated. Would the existence of a powerful Scottish Parliament weaken Scotland's links with the rest of the UK, possibly even to the extent of ending them? Was the setting up of the Parliament a symptom of some deeper drifting apart between Scotland and its neighbours, so that the Parliament was not the cause of constitutional disintegration so much as the means by which it might come about?

Using the survey data, we examine how views about the Parliament evolved in the first year of its operation, a period of intense controversy surrounding it (Chapter 6). There were disputes about the ending of student tuition fees, about the scrapping of a law that banned the 'promotion' in schools of homosexuality as an acceptable family form, and about the pay, standards and conduct of elected representatives. Although a great deal of this controversy in the printed media presented the members of the Parliament in a rather bad light, it did nevertheless ensure that the new body was at the centre of political attention. Did that mean that the UK Parliament in Westminster was becoming irrelevant to people in

Scotland? However imperfect the Scottish legislature may have seemed to be, was it seen by people in Scotland as the body that would lead the nation in the future? In that case, what future was there for Scotland's ties with the rest of the UK?

Part of the answer to these questions depends on how people in Scotland see the UK political system as a whole (Chapter 7). When Tony Blair's government was first elected in 1997, survey research suggested that his victory might have restored some optimism about politics, reversed a rise in cynicism about politicians, and produced a more hopeful sense that the political process could achieve worthwhile things. Has that been sustained in Scotland? Did the Scottish Parliament begin to fulfil the hopes of some of its founders – notably Donald Dewar – that it would renew the ties that citizens have with the state? Is having faith in the UK political system at odds with having faith in the emerging Scottish one, or do people tend to be optimistic or cynical about both?

Another part of the answer to the question about Scotland's ties with the rest of the UK is about policy (Chapter 9). Part of the rationale for setting up a Scottish Parliament has always been a claim that Scottish policy preferences are different from those in the rest of the UK, or at least from those in England. Yet previous survey research has shown repeatedly that, on most although not all matters, views do not differ much between Scotland and England. Did the advent of the Parliament start to shift Scottish opinion further away from opinion in England? Might that have been particularly true of opinion in relation to matters where the Parliament and Executive have been pursuing a distinctly different policy from the UK Government – such as over student tuition fees? Are views on matters that are the remit of the UK Parliament more similar to those in England than views on matters where the Scottish Parliament is free to pursue its own ideas?

Some of these topics also have implications for the internal social ties that constitute Scottish society, notably the question of attitudes to the political system. But many of these social ties are not directly political in a formal, public sense. At the most general level, there is the question of how much people interact with each other, how much they trust each other, and how strong are the moral principles by which they lead their lives (Chapter 2). These attributes are now frequently referred to as 'social capital', and we investigate its extent in Scotland, how that compares with the situation in England, and what its political consequences are. In particular, we assess the claim made famous by the US political scientist Robert Putnam that societies with abundant social capital are healthier democracies (in the sense that their citizens are more optimistic about politics), are more engaged with each other and with the political system, and are optimistic about the capacity of the political system to reform itself in worthwhile ways.

We look in detail at attitudes towards questions of personal morality, and at attitudes towards marriage, parenthood, sexuality and religion (Chapters 3, 4 and 5). Social institutions such as marriage and religion that have traditionally been prominent features of Scottish social life – as in all other European societies – are now weakening. But what implications do people see in this decline? Are our attitudes towards sexuality changing? The Scottish Parliament is now responsible for establishing the legal framework surrounding these and other moral matters, and the debate over homosexuality showed how intense the controversies can be when Parliament tries to shape social norms.

The final aspect of Scotland's ties that we examine is the country's regional diversity (Chapter 8). Scotland has always been regarded as a nation that has strong regional identities, and before 1997 these were often used by the opponents of a Scottish Parliament as a reason not to have one: it was claimed that a Parliament would be too dominated by the concerns of the most populous parts of the country, and so would pay inadequate attention to rural areas or areas distant from Edinburgh and Glasgow. Are there significant regional differences in attitudes to the topics that are covered in this book – politics, the constitution, social capital, personal morality, marriage, sexuality? Can any differences which are found be explained by different regions' having different demographic structures – for example, by the greater than average proportions of older people in the Borders, and of working-class people or Catholics in west-central Scotland?

The Scottish Social Attitudes Survey, on which our analysis of these questions is based, was conducted in summer 2000 by the National Centre for Social Research Scotland. This was the second survey in what is intended to become an annual series designed to provide an independent and authoritative account of what people in Scotland want from and feel about their new institutions. The Scottish Parliament cannot provide 'Scottish solutions to Scottish problems' unless we know what people in Scotland think the country's problems are and how they might be solved. The results of the first survey, conducted just after the 1999 election to the Scottish Parliament, were reported by Paterson et al (2001).

Many of these issues are about how Scotland is changing over time and how far it is different from the rest of the United Kingdom. We are able to compare many of the results of our survey with those of similar surveys that have been conducted in Scotland in the past and others that have been undertaken in the rest of Britain. The previous Scottish surveys are the 1997 Scottish Referendum Survey, and the Scottish Election Surveys of 1997, 1992 and 1979. Information on attitudes in England or England and Wales comes from the British Social Attitudes Surveys (Park et al 2001) together with the British Election Surveys. None of these surveys is designed to replicate opinion polls. They are not intended to map the latest reaction to recent political developments. They aim to chart long-term trends in what people think. It should be borne in mind that the data we are reporting here were collected in the summer of 2000. We hope that what we lose in immediacy is more than compensated for by what we provide in depth.

ACKNOWLEDGEMENT

The Scottish Social Attitudes survey was financed by the UK Economic and Social Research Council (grant number R000238065). We are grateful to the council for its support. We would also like to thank colleagues at the National Centre for Social Research – especially Kerstin Hinds and Katarina Thomson – for their advice during the project, and Ann Mair of the Social Statistics Laboratory, Strathclyde University for her work in preparing the data. The preparation of the book was greatly helped by the copy-editing of Sandra Scott, and the editors are indebted to her for her work. Our biggest debt is to the over 1600 people living in Scotland who freely gave us of their time and their views, without which this project would not have been possible at all.

REFERENCES

Park, A., Curtice, J., Thomson, K., Jarvis, L. and Bromley, C. (eds) (2001), *British Social Attitudes: the 18th report*, London: Sage.
Paterson, L., Brown, A., Curtice, J., Hinds, K., McCrone, D., Park, A., Sproston, K. and Surridge, P. (2001), *New Scotland, New Politics?*, Edinburgh: Edinburgh University Press.

2

SOCIAL CAPITAL AND CONSTITUTIONAL REFORM

LINDSAY PATERSON

INTRODUCTION

One of the boldest theories of political and constitutional change to have been advanced in recent decades is the claim that there is a link between social capital and political renewal, made first by Robert Putnam (1993) and frequently reiterated by him (Putnam 2001) and by many others (see the compendium of essays edited by Baron et al (2000)). Social capital, in this thesis, refers to the norms, trust and networks which constitute civil society (Coleman 1988). Although, in analytical practice, the concept seems not to differ much from classic ideas about what civil society is (Paterson 2000; Portes 1998), it does nevertheless appear to have a new relevance as levels of political participation and perhaps of social trust have declined. Putnam's argument is, essentially, that democracy itself requires strong reservoirs of social capital:

> the performance of representative government is facilitated by the social infrastructure of civic communities and by the democratic values of both officials and citizens. (Putnam 1993: 182).

Democracy depends on everyone trusting each other, and is facilitated if people are members of many kinds of social organisation. According to Putnam, they learn there how to work with others, they acquire confidence to take part in explicitly political

5

activities, and they develop a constructively critical attitude to the ways in which power is exercised.

In the United Kingdom before the Labour government embarked on its programme of constitutional reform in 1997, the Putnam thesis seemed to have very direct relevance to what many people felt was an over-centralised and undemocratic state. The source of renewal for that state would be civil society: a constitutional revolution from below would be more genuine, long-lasting, and democratic than anything imposed from above. The organisation Charter 88 became the embodiment of this kind of argument – the view that a strong civil society could underpin constitutional renewal and could then be strengthened by it. Academic respectability has then come in abundance, much of it drawing on the writing of Habermas (for example, Habermas 1984).

In Scotland, a similar programme underpinned the work of the Constitutional Convention between 1989 and 1995, producing the scheme that became the Labour government's proposals for a Scottish Parliament and that was popularly endorsed by the referendum in 1997. Arguments based on social capital appealed to reformers in the non-nationalist centre ground of politics, people such as Donald Dewar, John Smith and Gordon Brown in the Labour Party, and Menzies Campbell and Jim Wallace in the Liberal Democrats. According to this view, the Scottish Parliament would be a partner with civil society, owing its origins to civil society through the Convention, achieving its referendum endorsement because almost no segment of civil society opposed the idea in 1997, and working with civil society between 1997 and 1999 to agree a democratic and open way of operating. Now that the Parliament has been in place for over two years, the one area of its activity which has generally been regarded as a clear success – and as much more effective and democratic than Westminster – is the system of committees, seeking to produce consensual reform by consulting widely among civic bodies. Ultimately, indeed, the hope of these reformers has been that the good example shown in Scotland by founding a Parliament in the social capital of civil society would encourage the rest of the UK to go in the same direction.

Nevertheless, despite this enthusiasm for social capital, there have also been doubts. Portes (1998), for example, has pointed to a conceptual confusion in the dominant writing on the subject – a confusion between social capital as ethically neutral networks, and social capital as the moral content that might be gained from such ties. There is an analogous distinction drawn by critics of unalloyed enthusiasm for civil society (Hearn forthcoming). Civil society can be a scientific description of the civic institutions that organise social life, or it can be a moral ideal – an idea of how social life ought to be organised. The point of these critiques is that dense networks and strong civic organisations need not produce democratically respectable behaviour and ideas. The classic instance often given is of the Mafia, possessed of abundant social capital, a well-organised part of civil society (in the scientific sense), and yet an impediment to any kind of democratic renewal. A less graphic but more widely relevant example would be liberal doubts about strong communitarianism, a feeling that norms may be too strong for the good of liberal democracy (Feinberg 1998; Gray 1995). It could be that, in Granovetter's terminology, democracy depends more on weak ties than on strong ones (Granovetter 1973).

Examples of the problems which a strong civil society creates for politics can be found in the Netherlands in the middle of the twentieth century and in Northern Ireland currently. The Dutch state was organised into 'pillars' defined by religion to such an extent that people could lead almost their entire lives in a Protestant or in a Catholic social environment. As a result, the scope for truly autonomous state action was limited: initiatives for social reform could come only from within the pillars (Goudsblom 1968; Lijphart 1968). The difficulties of establishing a functioning politics in Northern Ireland are well known: the strength of organised interest groups has repeatedly frustrated attempts to make political institutions work, and the outcome of the present political process remains very uncertain (O'Leary 1999).

These are extreme examples, but there is a partial analogy to this questioning of the value of civil society in debates about the Scottish constitution. Some writers have denied that a strong Scottish civil society – strong indigenous social capital – need lead to support for a Scottish Parliament. It may be argued that an autonomous civil society has been, historically, precisely an alternative to a Parliament rather than a precursor to it. Now that civil society actually has produced a Parliament, this line of argument would question whether a Parliament with such origins will have the capacity to challenge civil society when that is needed: it may be too much under civil society's influence, too tied into networks of consultation to impose necessary reform.

This argument is then taken further by nationalist writers, notably by Tom Nairn (1997). A Scottish Parliament, they argue, would be no better than an emanation of civil society if it remained anchored in the networks of social capital. A truly popular Parliament must challenge the allegedly complacent elites of civil society, becoming the voice of the dispossessed and the marginalised against the complacency of conservative social institutions. There is an echo here of a familiar Marxist description of the state as a committee of the bourgeoisie, and, if we use the German term *bürgerlich* instead, the two arguments coincide: the whole problem with civil society is that it is run by the bourgeoisie, however politely and well-intentionedly, and however ameliorative its gradual social reforms might be, and is no substitute for a popular revolution against civil society, against social capital (see, for example, the discussion of Habermas's ideas by Cohen and Arato 1992: 220-31). Put differently, the solidarity of workers, or the solidarity of the nation, are the only politically efficacious ways of truly democratising the state.

Not all these issues may be resolved with data, but some can, because several of them are implicitly about whether and how certain kinds of political and social attitudes cluster together, and whether these clusterings are or are not supportive of particular kinds of constitutional reform. The chapter is in five further sections:

- First there is a description of various measures of social capital that are available from the 2000 Scottish and British Social Attitudes Surveys. We use these to compare the stocks of social capital in Scotland and England.
- Then there is a brief description of the analytical statistical methods that we use in the rest of the chapter.
- Next we look at the empirical question raised by Portes's distinction between empty and normative versions of social capital: is it in fact the case that people who belong to dense networks of organisations actually have benign views about society as a whole?
- Then we examine the relationship of political ideology to both the neutral and the normative definitions of social capital: are people in dense networks, and people who trust each other, really political reformers?
- The last section is the crux of the chapter: is social capital associated with a belief that the UK state in general, or the

Scottish governing system in particular, is in need of reform, and are the Scottish reforms that are currently being put in place appealing to any such social-capital-based beliefs? On the other hand, is there really the basis in popular views for the distinction drawn between the Labour or Liberal reformers who would anchor the Scottish Parliament in civil society, and the nationalist or socialist radicals who would want the Parliament to challenge civil society?

SOCIAL CAPITAL IN SCOTLAND AND ENGLAND

Any measures of social capital that can be collected by means of large-scale surveys inevitably appear somewhat trivial and arbitrary, especially so far as trust and norms are concerned. The Scottish and British Social Attitudes Surveys followed common practice in this regard. Trust was measured by asking people how they would behave towards neighbours or strangers in specific situations. Social norms, likewise, were measured by asking people for their views about the ethical acceptability of certain actions. Networks were measured by recording the length of time people had lived in their current neighbourhood, and by their membership of several different kinds of organisation. And then the character of people's membership of neighbourhoods or of organisations was assessed by asking how active they were in them. The results for Scotland and for England are shown in Tables 2.1 to 2.9. Since it is not the main purpose of this chapter to describe levels of social capital – but rather to investigate the social and ideological consequences of social capital – only a short summary of the measures is given here.

Table 2.1 asks about three everyday incidents that might tell us how much people trust their immediate neighbours. Large proportions of people would be comfortable with asking a neighbour to collect a medical prescription for them or for help in solving a simple household problem, but rather lower proportions would extend that trust to asking to borrow money. In each case, levels of trust were slightly higher in Scotland than in England.

A similar pattern can be seen for more general social trust in Table 2.2. Just under one half of people in Scotland and in England generally trust people, large majorities would ask a stranger for directions, and slight majorities would ask a stranger for change (the question specified of a £5 note). On trust, then, there seems to be a great deal of it around.

Table 2.1 Neighbourhood trust, Scotland and England, 2000

percentage	Scotland	England
Trust neighbour to collect prescription		
very comfortable	58	52
fairly comfortable	25	26
fairly uncomfortable	9	10
very uncomfortable	8	11
Ask neighbour for help to unblock sink		
very comfortable	62	59
fairly comfortable	27	26
fairly uncomfortable	5	7
very uncomfortable	5	7
Borrow money from neighbour to pay milkman		
very comfortable	22	20
fairly comfortable	15	15
fairly uncomfortable	16	17
very uncomfortable	45	46
Sample size	1663	1928

Don't know and not answered included in base.

Percentages are weighted; sample sizes are unweighted.

Source: Scottish Social Attitudes Survey 2000; British Social Attitudes Survey 2000.

On norms, Table 2.3 shows that people's sense of what is right does seem to depend on whether the transaction in question is with an identifiable other person or with an impersonal branch of the state. Cheating a shopkeeper out of change is firmly disapproved of by over four out of five people. Not declaring earnings in cash is rejected by about one half of respondents, and paying someone else cash to avoid tax is disapproved of only by minorities of about four in ten.

Table 2.2 General social trust, Scotland and England, 2000

percentage	Scotland	England
Social trust		
most people can be trusted	46	43
you can't be too careful	54	56
Ask stranger for directions		
very comfortable	47	51
fairly comfortable	40	38
fairly uncomfortable	10	8
very uncomfortable	3	3
Ask stranger for change to make phone call		
very comfortable	18	21
fairly comfortable	35	36
fairly uncomfortable	24	26
very uncomfortable	21	17
Sample size	1663	1928

Don't know and not answered included in base.

Percentages are weighted; sample sizes are unweighted.

Source: Scottish Social Attitudes Survey 2000; British Social Attitudes Survey 2000.

Table 2.4 shows that people in Scotland have generally lived somewhat longer in their current neighbourhood than people in England. On the other hand, according to Tables 2.5 and 2.6, most people do not join things, and, when they do, they tend to choose organisations that are local not national or international. Trade union membership is shown separately here (and is analysed separately later) because, during the first part of the twentieth century, unions were a means of incorporating into civil society those social groups who were potentially excluded from it; the question is then whether they continue to play such an including role. Table 2.6 shows that levels of union membership – including both trade unions and staff associations – are similar in Scotland and England, at around one fifth of the population (or about 30 per

11

cent of people in paid work). When union membership is included with the general membership of national and international organisations, the proportion who belong to nothing falls to 69 per cent in Scotland and to 65 per cent in England.

Table 2.3 General social norms, Scotland and England, 2000

percentage	Scotland	England
Keep wrong change in shop		
nothing wrong	3	4
bit wrong	10	12
wrong	47	48
seriously wrong	23	22
very seriously wrong	18	15
Not declare cash earnings		
nothing wrong	18	21
bit wrong	28	28
wrong	39	35
seriously wrong	8	10
very seriously wrong	6	5
Pay cash to avoid VAT		
nothing wrong	26	29
bit wrong	30	31
wrong	33	27
seriously wrong	8	8
very seriously wrong	3	4
Sample size	1663	1928

Don't know and not answered included in base.

Percentages are weighted; sample sizes are unweighted.

Source: Scottish Social Attitudes Survey 2000; British Social Attitudes Survey 2000.

Table 2.4 Length of residence in neighbourhood, Scotland and England, 2000

percentage	Scotland	England
0-5 years	24	29
6-16 years	27	28
17-30 years	26	23
31 or more years	23	19
Sample size	1663	1928

Don't know and not answered included in base.

Percentages are weighted; sample sizes are unweighted.

Source: Scottish Social Attitudes Survey 2000; British Social Attitudes Survey 2000.

Table 2.5 Membership of local organisations, Scotland and England, 2000

percentage	Scotland	England
Organisations in general*		
none	78	73
one	18	20
two or more	4	6
Sports and cultural groups		
none	73	75
sports only	22	18
cultural only	4	5
both	2	2
Sample size	1663	1928

* Tenants' or residents' association; parents' association; school board; political party; community council or local council; neighbourhood council or forum; Neighbourhood Watch Scheme; local conservation or environmental group; or other local community or voluntary group.

Don't know and not answered included in base.

Percentages are weighted; sample sizes are unweighted.

Source: Scottish Social Attitudes Survey 2000; British Social Attitudes Survey 2000.

Table 2.6 Membership of national and international organisations, and trade unions, Scotland and England, 2000

percentage	Scotland	England
national and international organisations*		
none	85	82
one	11	13
two or more	3	5
member of trade union or staff association	20	22
Sample size	1663	1928

*National Trust for Scotland or for England and Wales; Royal Society for the Protection of Birds; Friends of the Earth; World Wildlife Fund or Worldwide Fund for Nature; Greenpeace; Association for the Protection of Rural Scotland or England; other wildlife or countryside protection group; Ramblers Association; other countryside sport or recreation group; urban conservation group; Campaign for Nuclear Disarmament.

Don't know and not answered included in base.

Percentages are weighted; sample sizes are unweighted.

Source: Scottish Social Attitudes Survey 2000; British Social Attitudes Survey 2000.

Table 2.7 Neighbourhood activism, Scotland and England, 2000

percentage	Scotland	England
Help old woman being harassed by young people		
definitely help	57	54
probably help	34	38
probably not help	7	6
definitely not help	2	2
Sample size	1663	1928

Don't know and not answered included in base.

Percentages are weighted; sample sizes are unweighted.

Source: Scottish Social Attitudes Survey 2000; British Social Attitudes Survey 2000.

Table 2.8 Political activism, Scotland and England, 2000

percentage	Scotland	England
Number of political actions[*] in protest at government action		
none	40	48
one	39	33
two	12	11
three	5	5
four or more	4	4
Sample size	1663	1928

[*] *Contacted an MSP or MP; spoke to an influential person; contacted a government department; contacted a radio or TV station or a newspaper; signed a petition; raised an issue in an organisation to which the respondent already belonged; gone on a protest or demonstration; formed a group of like-minded people.*

Don't know and not answered included in base.

Percentages are weighted; sample sizes are unweighted.

Source: Scottish Social Attitudes Survey 2000; British Social Attitudes Survey 2000.

Most people would help an old woman who was being harassed by youths (Table 2.7), but levels of other kinds of activism were small, as Tables 2.8 and 2.9 show. The apparently higher instance of political activism (Table 2.8) is accounted for by signing petitions, which was done by 50 per cent of people in Scotland and 41 per cent of people in England. Other kinds of political action were carried out by 17 per cent of people in Scotland and by 18 per cent of people in England.

ANALYTICAL METHODS

Before we investigate whether and how trust, norms and actions relate to each other, we summarise the disparate questions on trust and norms into a smaller number of scales, because some groups of questions turn out to be telling us much the same thing: in technical terms, groups of questions are quite strongly correlated with each other. The different dimensions of trust and norms can be detected by factor analysis (see Appendix to the book): the technical details of this do not matter here, since it is simply being used to find out how the questions shown in Tables 2.1, 2.2 and 2.3 relate to each other. In both Scotland and England, there were essentially five dimensions, three for trust and two for norms, leading to the following scales which we use in all subsequent analysis:

NEIGHBOURHOOD TRUST

This grouped the three questions in Table 2.1. The response options were assigned numerical values (for example, 1 for 'very comfortable') and then the three of these were added up for each respondent. Thus, on this scale, low values mean high levels of trust.

COMMUNITY TRUST

This grouped the two questions about strangers in Table 2.2. A scale was derived in the same way as for neighbourhood trust. So low values mean high trust.

GENERAL SOCIAL TRUST

This dimension was simply the first question in Table 2.2. Again, then, low values mean high trust.

NEIGHBOURHOOD NORM

This was the first question in Table 2.3, concerning keeping wrong change from a shop. So high values mean a strong norm.

GENERAL SOCIAL NORM

This grouped the second and third questions in Table 2.3, relating to evading tax. The scale was created by adding together the responses to the two questions, and so, again, high values indicate a strong norm.

These five trust and norm variables, along with length of residence in the neighbourhood (Table 2.4), were then used in multiple regressions to predict the variables that are of primary interest in each of the subsequent sections – membership and action in the next section, political ideology in the following one, and views about the constitution in the final one. (Multiple regression is described more fully in the Appendix.) For ideology and for the constitution, measures of membership and of action are also included in the regressions to test whether they and the trust and norms variables might have independent influences. The rest of the chapter summarises the consistent results to emerge from a large number of regression analyses of this type. The details of the regressions are not what matter here: the important point for the political and academic theories outlined in the Introduction to the chapter is whether social capital is associated with various views about politics, society and the constitution, and, if so, whether the direction of these associations is consistent with the claims made by Putnam and by Scottish constitutional reformers.

Table 2.9 Volunteering, Scotland and England, 2000

percentage	Scotland	England
Political activities in past year		
none	97	96
once or twice	3	3
three or more times	1	1
Charitable activities in past year		
none	76	77
once or twice	15	13
three to five times	4	3
six or more times	6	7
Church-related activities in past year		
none	86	85
once or twice	7	6
three to five times	2	3
six or more times	6	6
Other voluntary activities in past year		
none	80	80
once or twice	10	9
three to five times	2	3
six or more times	8	8
Sample size	1523	1553

Don't know and not answered included in base.

Percentages are weighted; sample sizes are unweighted.

Source: Scottish Social Attitudes Survey 2000; British Social Attitudes Survey 2000.

We also investigate whether any associations remain after taking account of demographic characteristics. The matters we pay attention to are age, sex, religious affiliation, social class, and education level. For example, if we find (as we do) that both trust and membership levels are higher among the better educated, is any association between trust and membership levels solely because of that, or are trust and membership levels associated with each other even at given levels of education?

Most of the remainder of the discussion is of Scotland, but where comparison was possible (that is, on matters that were asked about in the surveys in both England and Scotland) the conclusions for England were mostly similar to those for Scotland.

TRUST, NORMS AND ACTION

The first question is to test whether trust and norms are related to levels of membership and inclinations to activism – that is, to the variables in Tables 2.5, 2.6, 2.7, 2.8 and 2.9. For this analysis, the numbers of memberships (Tables 2.5 and 2.6) were treated as simple counts (trade union membership continuing to be dealt with separately), the inclination to help an old woman being harassed (Table 2.7) was treated as a scale, the number of protest actions (Table 2.8) was also treated as a count, and the numbers of voluntary activities (Table 2.9) were summarised into a single scale with points 'none', 'at least one type of activity on 1-2 occasions', 'at least one type of activity on 3-5 occasions', and 'at least one type of activity on 6 or more occasions'.

There were indeed clear links between norms and trust on the one hand and membership and action on the other. Levels of neighbourhood trust (Table 2.1) were associated with membership and with all types of action. That is, people who were more trusting were more likely to be members of local organisations, and of national and international organizations; were more likely to say they would help an old woman; were more likely to have undertaken voluntary activity; and were more likely to have engaged in political protest. The other two dimensions of trust (Table 2.2) were associated with some although not all of these things. Likewise, holding a strong set of norms (Table 2.3) was associated with being a member of national or international organisations, with helping an old woman, and with carrying out many voluntary actions. Length of residence was generally not associated with anything, but

18

having been in the neighbourhood for a long time was associated with undertaking fewer protest actions. Union membership was associated with the same kinds of things as other kinds of membership: more trusting people were more likely to be in a union than less trusting people.

These conclusions were not explained by demographic characteristics. Several of the demographic variables – notably measuring education – were associated with the measures of trust, and of norms, and were also associated with numbers of memberships and with levels of activism. But none of these demographic variables accounted for the association between trusts and norms on the one hand and memberships or activism on the other. Thus, even at given levels of education, people who were more trusting were more likely to be a member of various organisations and were more likely to engage in various types of social action.

Because we do not have longitudinal data, we cannot say what the causal processes are. It is quite possible, for example, that people become more trusting, or develop stronger norms, by joining organisations, or by taking part in voluntary activism. It is alternatively possible that trust and norms induce them to join or to be active. Almost certainly, both directions of causation are in operation. Nevertheless, we can now answer the first question posed earlier. Although Portes's distinction between amoral networks and what is taken from these networks is useful analytically, it is clear that, in Scotland, networks are associated with norms and trust in the ways predicted by Putnam and others. It does then seem useful and not too simplifying to refer to the whole nexus of trust, norms and networks by the singular term social capital.

SOCIAL CAPITAL AND POLITICAL IDEOLOGY

The main topic of this chapter, however, is not the description of social capital but an investigation of its possible political consequences. So the next step is to test the propositions that many political reformers have advanced over the last couple of decades. Are people with large amounts of social capital – whether norms, trust or networks – less cynical about the political system? Moreover, what kinds of ideology do they show? Do people with large quantities of social capital tend to be liberal, and are they inclined to favour constitutional and social reform?

Political cynicism is measured in the survey by four questions, asking people whether they agree that it makes little difference which parties win elections, and that politicians tend to lose touch with voters, tend to be more interested in votes than in voters' views, and tend to be uninterested in the views of ordinary people. These questions are discussed more fully elsewhere in the book (especially Chapter 7). For present purposes, they are constructed into a scale as described in the book's Appendix. This scale is sometimes referred to elsewhere as measuring 'political efficacy', but since the questions do not in fact refer directly to individuals' efficacy of the type with which we are concerned in this chapter, a less confusing label here is as a scale running from cynicism at one end to faith in the political system at the other.

The other two dimensions of ideology that are used are also described in the book's Appendix. There is a scale measuring the respondent's position on a dimension running from left to right, and another scale similarly measuring views as between libertarianism and authoritarianism.

Multiple regression was used to see whether and how the scales were associated with the measures of trust, norms and activism that make up social capital. On the cynicism-political-faith scale, the results were exactly as the theses of Putnam and others would predict. People who evinced low levels of cynicism tended to be more socially trusting, to have strong social norms, to be members of numerous organisations, and to have engaged in many political and voluntary actions.

Although – as have seen – trust and norms were associated with membership and action, all of these were independently associated with low levels of cynicism. So, whether levels of trust and norms precede levels of membership and action, or vice versa, we can say that high trust and strong norms are directly associated with low cynicism, and also that intense membership and action are also associated with low cynicism. Of course, the possibility of reverse causation also arises here. It is possible that people who are inclined not to be cynical about politics infer from that a high level of general social trust. Nevertheless, that does seem less likely, because it implies that most people are motivated first by views about the political system. It is more likely that general social trust etc come first, and that they then induce trust in governing institutions.

Trade union membership did not provide an alternative route to political faith for the otherwise inactive or distrusting: it was not associated with this scale at all.

However, on the two dimensions of political ideology, results conformed less to the standard assumptions of the Scottish liberal left. It is true that libertarian views go along with strong trust and with a tendency to be a member of many organisations. However, libertarianism also goes along with relatively weak social norms. Indeed, on the question about helping an old woman who was being harassed by young people, help was more likely to come from people with authoritarian views than from those with libertarian views. This is much more consistent with Portes's than with Putnam's propositions. Strong communitarianism is not necessarily liberal.

That is even starker on the left-right dimension. Here the picture is unambiguous: it is relatively right-wing ideology which goes along with high levels of trust, strong norms and intense membership (apart from trade union membership), although there is no association between this dimension and a propensity to be active politically. That is partly but by no means only because well-educated and well-off people tend to be more right wing and to have more social capital: the association between right wing views and high levels of social capital remains even among people with given levels of education or in a given social class.

And yet the apparent paradox here is resolved if we drop an assumption that all kinds of reformist politics need go together. It is clear that, in Scotland, social capital does underpin political engagement in precisely the way that Putnam suggests: high trust, strong norms and many memberships are associated with a resistance to political cynicism. Not all kinds of social capital support liberal views: trust and membership do, but strong norms do not. That may be what Granovetter would mean by the potency of weak ties. But where social capital definitely does not support social reform is in relation to standard issues between the ideological left and right. Strong social capital is associated with support for the existing social and economic order. The only kind of membership that was associated with left-wing views was – not surprisingly – belonging to a trade union.

SOCIAL CAPITAL AND CONSTITUTIONAL REFORM

For Scotland, this brings us to the nub of the matter. On the one hand, the Putnam thesis would tend to suggest that the movement for constitutional reform rested on strong social capital. Moreover, the establishment of the Scottish Parliament has also frequently been asserted to be an expression of an allegedly strong sense of community in Scotland – most famously in the Claim of Right in 1988 – and so presumably would go along with strong norms and trust. Yet, at the same time, we know from numerous previous studies that this movement also rested on quite left-wing foundations, if only because it was partly an expression of Scottish disenfranchisement under the Conservative government after 1979 (Mitchell 1996; Paterson 1998). Because we have found in the previous section that social capital does not relate to left-wing views in ways that would be consistent with most of the assumptions of Scottish constitutional reformers, we might now expect some complexity in the connections between social capital and views about the constitution. (Attitudes to the constitution themselves are discussed in more detail in Chapter 6.)

At first sight, the analysis does not confirm the Putnam thesis, or the campaigning ideas of liberal reformers in the Constitutional Convention and in Charter 88: social capital seems to be associated with faith in the UK constitution. People in Scotland who believed in 2000 that the UK constitution was working well were more socially trusting than people who were critical of it. Likewise, high levels of trust and a tendency to belong to a lot of organisations were associated with believing that the UK Parliament may be expected to represent Scotland's interests effectively, although social norms were not associated with views on this question. But, in fact, this may not be as contradictory of the liberal reformers' position after all, if respondents are judging the capacity of a devolved UK to support Scottish democracy. For it turns out that the same pattern of views and practices as seem to incline people to have faith in the UK constitution as a whole also now incline them to be optimistic about the Scottish Parliament. Thus believing that the Scottish Parliament would stand up for Scottish interests was associated with high levels of neighbourhood trust and of community trust. And high levels of trust were associated with an inclination to believe that the Scottish Parliament was giving people a greater say in government.

Trust was associated also with respect for at least one of the Scottish civic institutions that had maintained Scottish autonomy before the Parliament was established: possessing strong social capital was associated with believing that teachers and head teachers ought to be in charge of the day-to-day running of schools (for further discussion of which, see Chapter 9). And holding to strong social norms was associated with general support for the present home rule settlement in Scotland, as against either independence or a return to having no elected parliament at all (see also Chapter 6).

So there is a constituency of support for the liberal constitutional reformers, but it is not one that is otherwise disengaged from the political system. Those who tend to the view that the Scottish Parliament is renewing Scottish democracy tend also to be quite optimistic about the UK constitution, tend to be well-embedded in various social networks, and tend to evince a generally high level of social trust and to adhere to a generally strong set of social norms. They also tend to respect at least one of the civic institutions – school education – that safeguarded Scottish autonomy and identity in the Union before the Scottish Parliament was established.

But, of course, it was not these people whom the reformers were trying to engage with politics. This brings us back to one of the most controversial aspects of the debates that have been engendered by Putnam's analysis. Putnam himself tends to argue that building social capital is a necessary precursor of democratic reform, but constitutional reformers have also argued in the reverse direction – that constitutional reform can re-engage the disaffected, and can rebuild community and social trust. In Scotland, support for a Scottish Parliament has certainly come in part from this motive, and such arguments – as we noted – have been most popular among proponents of reform in the Labour movement and among Liberal Democrats. Alongside these arguments, however, has been nationalism.

And it turns out that nationalism in Scotland is now associated with much weaker levels of social capital than is characteristic of the liberal reformist position. Weak social capital is associated with people feeling strongly Scottish on a standard scale of national identity (the so-called Moreno scale, ranging from 'Scottish not British' at one end to 'British not Scottish' at the other). Strong social capital is, in Scotland, a characteristic of identifying as British. Weak trust, weak norms and low levels of membership are associated with perceiving a great deal of conflict between Scotland

and England, and with believing that England benefits disproportionately from the Union (for fuller details of which questions, see Paterson et al 2001: 116-7). Weak social capital is also associated with less trust in Scotland's civic institutions – less willingness to trust teachers to run schools. Less engagement with political activism, and weak trust and norms, are associated with wanting the powers of the Scottish Parliament to be extended (see also Chapter 6). And these same things are associated with preferring outright independence to home rule.

None of these differences were explained away by demography. For example, compared with working class people, the salariat tended to be more supportive of home rule, and of the maintenance of the UK, to feel less strongly Scottish, to be liberal and towards the right ideologically. As we noted earlier, salariat members also tended to have more social capital. But, even comparing two members of the salariat or two members of the working class, the one with the more social capital would be more supportive of home rule etc. Moreover, as earlier with political cynicism, trade union membership did not provide a way in which socially excluded people could engage with the political system or with devolution: union members were no more likely than non-members to support the current form of Scottish Parliament, or to have faith in the UK state to respond to Scottish needs.

The implications of all the stages in the analysis in this chapter are illustrated in detail in Tables 2.10 to 2.13 for two of the social capital variables – membership of national or international organisations (from Table 2.6) and general social trust (the first question in Table 2.2). Also shown there are a selection of ideological views, and some educational and social class characteristics.

Although a few of the differences associated with social capital are quite small, most are not, and the patterns are consistent. People who are members of organisations and who are trusting tend to view the UK constitution and the Scottish Parliament more benignly than people who are not. For example, the proportion believing that the Scottish Parliament works in Scotland's interests is 60 per cent among those who are generally trusting, but 52 per cent among those who are not (Table 2.12). The organised and the trusting are generally more sympathetic to home rule than those who are not (by 61 per cent to 54 per cent in relation to membership (Table 2.10), and by 57 per cent to 54 per cent for trust (Table 2.12)). So the reformed constitution of the UK as it operates in Scotland gains more support from people with a lot of social capital than from those who have less.

Table 2.10 Views about the governing system and Scotland, by membership of national and international organisations, Scotland, 2000

percentage	Membership of national or international organisations[1]	
	no membership	at least one membership
The UK constitution works well[2]	32	40
Trust UK government to work in Scotland's interests[3]	17	26
Trust Scottish Parliament to work in Scotland's interests[3]	55	58
Support home rule	54	61
Teachers should manage schools	59	64
More powers for Scottish Parliament	71	49
Support independence	32	19
Predominantly Scottish[4]	75	53
Conflict Scotland/England[5]	40	28
England benefits disproportionately from the Union	45	29
Sample size	1417	246

[1] *Derived from Table 2.6.*

[2] *'Works extremely well' or 'works mainly well'.*

[3] *'Just about always' or 'most of the time'.*

[4] *'Scottish not British' or 'Scottish more than British'.*

[5] *'Very serious' or 'fairly serious' conflict.*

Don't know and not answered included in base.

Percentages are weighted; sample sizes are unweighted.

Source: Scottish Social Attitudes Survey 2000.

Table 2.11 Ideology and demographic characteristics, by membership of national and international organisations, Scotland, 2000

percentage	Membership of national or international organisations[1]	
	no membership	at least one membership
Ideology		
Members of parliament lose touch[2]	64	54
There is one law for the rich and one for the poor[2]	70	50
Criminals should be given stiffer sentences[2]	81	71
Demographic characteristics		
Higher education qualification	25	54
No qualifications	34	13
Salariat	24	53
Working class	32	10
Sample size	1417	246

[1] *Derived from Table 2.6.*

[2] *'Agree strongly' or 'agree'.*

Don't know and not answered included in base.

Percentages are weighted; sample sizes are unweighted.

Source: Scottish Social Attitudes Survey 2000.

Those with abundant social capital tend to be less cynical about politicians: 54 per cent of people who are members of organisations agreed that politicians lose touch, compared with 64 per cent of those who are not members (Table 2.11); the proportions agreeing strongly were 21 per cent and 28 per cent. People with social capital tend to be more optimistic about social inequalities: 50 per cent of people who are members agree that there is 'one law for the rich and one for the poor', in contrast to 70 per cent of those who are not members (Table 2.11). And they tend to be less illiberal: 71 per cent of members believe criminals should receive stiffer sentences, compared to 81 per cent of people who are not members (Table

2.11). The patterns on these ideological dimensions are similar though less pronounced in relation to social trust (Table 2.13).

Table 2.12 Views about the governing system and Scotland, by levels of social trust, Scotland, 2000

percentage	general social trust[1]	
	you can't be too careful	most people can be trusted
The UK constitution works well[2]	30	38
Trust UK government to work in Scotland's interests[3]	17	20
Trust Scottish Parliament to work in Scotland's interests[3]	52	60
Support home rule	54	57
Teachers should manage schools	57	63
More powers for Scottish Parliament	73	61
Support independence	31	29
Predominantly Scottish[4]	74	69
Conflict Scotland/England[5]	46	29
England benefits disproportionately from the Union	43	41
Sample size	908	740

[1] First question shown in Table 2.2.

[2] 'Works extremely well' or 'works mainly well'.

[3] 'Just about always' or 'most of the time'.

[4] 'Scottish not British' or 'Scottish more than British'.

[5] 'Very serious' or 'fairly serious' conflict.

Don't know and not answered included in base.

Percentages are weighted; sample sizes are unweighted.

Source: Scottish Social Attitudes Survey 2000.

Table 2.13 Ideology and demographic characteristics, by levels of social trust, Scotland, 2000

	general social trust[1]	
percentage	you can't be too careful	most people can be trusted
Ideology		
Members of parliament lose touch[2]	67	58
There is one law for the rich and one for the poor[2]	72	61
Criminals should be given stiffer sentences[2]	82	76
Demographic characteristics		
Higher education qualification	22	37
No qualifications	36	24
Salariat	20	37
Working class	35	21
Sample size	908	740

[1] *First question shown in Table 2.2.*

[2] *'Agree strongly' or 'agree'.*

Don't know and not answered included in base.

Percentages are weighted; sample sizes are unweighted.

Source: Scottish Social Attitudes Survey 2000.

People with social capital tend to be well educated and middle class. For example, 54 per cent of those who are members of organisations have a higher education qualification, in contrast to 25 per cent of those who are not (Table 2.11). Moreover, trade union membership does not compensate. People with general social capital also tend to be more likely than those without social capital to be in a trade union (by 25 per cent to 19 per cent on membership of national organisations, and by 22 per cent to 18 per cent on general social trust).

But wanting further reform of the Scottish constitution is associated with quite opposite characteristics. More powers for the Scottish Parliament are favoured by 71 per cent of those who are not members of organisations, but only 49 per cent of those who are members (Table 2.10). People who are not members tend to be more Scottish in their chosen identity than those who are members (75 per cent against 53 per cent: Table 2.10). They are more likely to perceive conflict between Scotland and England (40 per cent against 28 per cent) and to believe that England benefits disproportionately from the Union (45 per cent against 29 per cent). Similar, although generally weaker, patterns are found in relation to social trust (Table 2.12).

CONCLUSIONS

During the referendum in 1997, a very effective coalition was established, between liberal reformers mainly in the Labour Party and the Liberal Democrats on the one hand, and nationalists mainly in the Scottish National Party on the other. This worked in the sense that it brought together two quite different arguments for a Scottish Parliament, the split between which had fatally undermined the campaigns in the earlier referendum in 1979. One of these arguments owed a great deal to the kind of case that has been put forward by Putnam and others. It argued that constitutional reform was needed to renew democracy, not only in Scotland but throughout the UK. It tended to be associated ideologically with liberal views on many other issues, and, in the Labour Party, it tended to be linked to the non-ideological centrism that Tony Blair has enthusiastically espoused (and which is analysed in Chapter 9). The other argument in the referendum was not, at that time, necessarily in tension with the first. It was essentially nationalist. It argued for a Scottish Parliament to empower the people of Scotland (conceived collectively but nearly always in pluralistic, civic ways, not ethnically), and it tended also to be associated with quite strongly socialist or social democratic commitments.

The liberal reformist case for home rule was crucial in attracting middle class support. Indeed, the conversion of the middle class to home rule at the same time as they were growing in size was the crucial social and political change between 1979 and 1997. In the earlier referendum (according to the 1979 Scottish Election Survey), the middle class, meaning people in non-manual occupations, made up one third of the electorate. Only 40 per cent of them voted in favour of a Scottish Assembly. In 1997 (in the Scottish Referendum Survey), the middle class constituted nearly two thirds of the

29

electorate, and voted 69 per cent in favour. That was as large a swing as in the working class (which went from 57 per cent in favour to 91 per cent), but had more momentous political consequences: it delivered the clear majority for home rule. If the middle class had remained at their 1979 levels of support, while still growing in size as they did, the overall proportion in favour of a Scottish Parliament in 1997 would have been only 58 per cent, not 74 per cent.

Now that the Scottish Parliament has been established, it appears from the analysis here that this temporary coalition built up over two decades may be beginning to come apart. There are now emerging two distinct popular perceptions of what the Scottish Parliament is for, what it is doing, and where it might be going. One – taking forward the liberal reformism – sees it as a means of renewing liberal democracy, finds the best way of doing that in closely embedding the parliament in civil society, and inclines to the belief that both the parliament and the UK state are potentially benign. This view tends to support libertarian causes, and is on the whole not strongly socialist. It is a view that tends to be held by people who are already thoroughly embedded in social networks, who generally trust other people, and who hold to strong social norms. These people, while holding a clearly Scottish identity, are willing also to acknowledge an attachment to Britishness. They tend to be well-educated and to be in good jobs. Perhaps a not inappropriate description of their typical views would then be bourgeois constitutionalism.

The other view points in quite different directions, and is held by quite different kinds of people. For them, the Scottish Parliament is a means of challenging the Union, challenging the civil society that has maintained Scotland's place in the Union, and, if not challenging the capitalist social order, then wanting some fairly strong measures of social democratic reform. This view is not particularly libertarian. It is held by people who are not part of strong social networks – even trade unions – and who tend not to have a great deal of trust in others in general. It is held by people who are firmly Scottish in their cultural allegiance, and who have little education and occupy low-status jobs. It is, in other words, the view of the socially excluded, the very group whom the liberal reformers hoped that mere devolution – as opposed to independence – would re-engage.

So the main ideological antagonism in Scotland is now not, as it was in the 1980s and 1990s, between a reforming bloc that was both left-of-centre and dissatisfied with the UK constitution and a right-of-centre intransigence on decentralising power. Even less is the main tension now between nationalism and socialism, as it was for many Labour movement people in the 1970s and earlier. Socialism and nationalism have become aligned with each other at a popular level in Scotland, and both have become the preferred ideology of social outsiders. Abundant social capital may indeed incline people to decentralise the constitution, and to reform the capitalist social order moderately, but it is not now the main source of support for their being radically transformed.

REFERENCES

Baron, S., Field, J. and Schuller, T. (eds) (2000), *Social Capital: Social Theory and the Third Way*, Oxford: Oxford University Press.

Cohen, J. L. and Arato, A. (1992), *Civil Society and Political Theory*, Cambridge, Mass.: MIT Press.

Coleman, J. S. (1988), 'Social capital in the creation of human capital', *American Journal of Sociology*, 94, pp. s95-s119.

Feinberg, W. (1998), *Common Schools, Uncommon Identities*, New Haven: Yale University Press.

Goudsblom, J. (1968), *Dutch Society*, New York: Random House.

Granovetter, M. S. (1973), 'The strength of weak ties', *American Journal of Sociology*, 78, pp. 1360-80.

Gray, J. (1995), *Enlightenment's Wake*, London: Routledge.

Habermas, J. (1984), *The Theory of Communicative Action, Vol. I: Reason and the Rationalisation of Society*, London: Heinemann.

Hearn, J. S. (forthcoming), 'Introduction', in J. S. Hearn (ed.), *Taking Liberties: Contesting Visions of the Civil Society Project*, special issue of *Critique of Anthropology*.

Lijphart, A. (1968), *The Politics of Accommodation: Pluralism and Democracy in the Netherlands*, Berkeley: University of California Press.

Mitchell, J. (1996), *Strategies for Self-Government*, Edinburgh: Polygon.

Nairn, T. (1997), *Faces of Nationalism*, London: Verso.

O'Leary, B. (1999), 'The 1998 British-Irish agreement: power-sharing plus', *Scottish Affairs*, no. 26, winter, pp. 14-35.

Paterson, L. (1998), *A Diverse Assembly: the Debate on a Scottish Parliament*, Edinburgh University Press.

Paterson, L. (2000), 'Civil society and democratic renewal', in S. Baron, J. Field and T. Schuller (eds), *Social Capital: Social Theory and the Third Way*, Oxford: Oxford University Press, pp. 39-55.

Portes, A. (1998), 'Social capital: its origins and applications in modern sociology', *Annual Review of Sociology*, 24, pp. 1-24.

Putnam, R. D. (1993), *Making Democracy Work*, Princeton: Princeton University Press.

Putnam, R. D. (2001), *Bowling Alone: The Collapse and Revival of American Community*, New York: Simon and Schuster.

3

REJECTING TRADITIONAL FAMILY BUILDING? ATTITUDES TO COHABITATION AND TEENAGE PREGNANCY IN SCOTLAND

KERSTIN HINDS AND LYNN JAMIESON

INTRODUCTION

Everyday experiences of family life and personal relationships have changed significantly in recent decades. Trends in Scotland in how people move into and out of partnerships, in parenting arrangements, and in household structures, are very similar to trends in England, and indeed throughout 'Western' societies. Debate is international concerning whether such changes in family life are positive, or are serious social problems, symptomatic of a general moral malaise. Both views stimulate debate about what should be done, whether in terms of accommodating the new circumstances in which people live or seeking to reassert more traditional patterns.

This chapter explores the attitudes of people in Scotland towards two issues that attract considerable attention from the public, media and academics: cohabitation and teenage pregnancy. For those who wish to reassert more traditional patterns, both are seen to threaten a perceived social order, involving marriage and planned parenthood. Given the reality of changes in partnerships and family arrangements, it is important to understand public opinion on these matters. Does tolerance express an acceptance of change: either a resigned acknowledgement that social ties are fragmenting or a celebration of a perceived alternative social order? While this chapter focuses on attitudes to deviation from traditional family patterns, the following chapter examines, in detail, cohabitation, which members of society cohabit, and what the legal status is of cohabitation in Scotland.

Both cohabitation and teenage pregnancy are the subject of policy concern at the UK and Scottish level. Ambitious targets for cutting teenage pregnancy have been set – in Scotland the target is a reduction of 20 per cent of the pregnancy rate in 13-15 year olds by 2010. In England the aim is to reduce the pregnancy rate among those aged under 18 by 50 per cent over the same period. The legal rights of cohabitees and unmarried fathers have also been a subject of government interest and there is some indication of divergence in policy north and south of the border. As discussed in Chapter 4, Scottish proposals may result in more parity in the rights of married and unmarried couples in Scotland than in England and Wales.

The demographic trends in cohabitation and teenage pregnancy are very different. Cohabitation has risen sharply, becoming a common practice among young adults, but teenage pregnancy has remained a minority phenomenon.

The practice of cohabitation has risen steadily since the 1970s: between 1976 and 1998 the proportion of women under 50 who were cohabiting in Britain increased more than three-fold, from nine per cent to 29 per cent (Haskey 2001). In 1999 19 per cent of 25-34 year olds in Britain were cohabiting (General Household Survey 1998[1]). Looking just at Scotland, it can be seen that a lower proportion of this age group, 15 per cent, were cohabiting (Hope et al 2000: 22). While living together without being married is not entirely new, it has shifted rapidly from a minority practice to a typical way of forming a household as a couple (Ermisch and Francesconi 2000; Haskey 1999; Kiernan 1999).

The rise in cohabitation has been associated with a decline in the popularity of marriage – from a peak marriage rate in the 1960s and 1970s to a much lower marriage rate in the 1990s. In 1999 there were 36.7 first marriages per thousand unmarried women in Scotland whereas in 1989 just 10 years previously there were 51.7 marriages. Scotland has a slightly higher first marriage rate than England; about two more people per thousand marry for the first time in Scotland each year.

In both Scotland and England the average (mean) age on first marriage has risen over recent decades and in 2000 stood at 30.5 for men and 28.6 for women. Teenage marriage was much more common in the 1970s than it is today. The rise in the average age of marriage through the 1980s and 1990s has been partly due to people living together for a year or two before getting married. By the 1990s the majority of couples marrying for the first time had lived together before marriage (Haskey 1999). While some commentators fear that cohabitation is replacing marriage, John Ermisch argues that cohabitation has become part of the process of finding someone to marry (Ermisch 2000). Those who express concern at cohabitation would not necessarily encourage marriage at very young ages, regarding the teenage years as 'too young' for marriage and parenting.

Whether as an alternative to marriage or part of the process of marrying, the trend towards cohabitation has contributed to an increasing proportion of children being born outside of marriage. In England and Wales and in Scotland, about 40 per cent of all births are outside of marriage. However, the majority of these (over 70 per cent in Scotland and 60 per cent in England and Wales) are jointly registered by parents living at the same address. Nevertheless, opponents of cohabitation typically take the view that marriage is a more satisfactory arrangement for children (Morgan 1995).

Most teenage births in Scotland are outside of marriage and marriage is less commonly a response to unplanned pregnancy than in the 1970s or 1980s. In 1998, 95 per cent of all births to Scottish women under 20 were outside of marriage, compared with 41 per cent of all births. In England and Wales the proportion of teenage births outside marriage was slightly lower (89 per cent). The overall rates of birth to teenagers are not higher in Scotland than England (30 per 1000 women aged 15-19 in 1999 compared with 30.8 in England and Wales) but the birth rate among unmarried teenagers has been slightly higher since 1992 (28.8 births per 1000 unmarried women aged 15-19 in Scotland and 27.6 in England and Wales in 1999).

Not all pregnancies, of course, result in a birth. The abortion rate in the UK has risen since the 1967 Abortion Act, levelling off in the 1990s. While women of all reproductive ages have abortions, rates per thousand women are highest in the 16-19 and 20-24 age groups. The figures for the year 1999 are 11.2 abortions per 1000 women in Scotland aged 15-44, 20.6 per 1000 women aged 16-19 and 21.6 per 1000 women aged 20-24 (Abortion Act Statistics Scotland 2000). The percentage of teenage pregnancies resulting in an abortion among those who become pregnant at age 16-19 was 43 per cent in 1998. Among the small number of Scottish teenagers who become pregnant at age 13-15 (fewer than a thousand per year) about half of the pregnancies result in an abortion.

Rates of teenage pregnancy in Scotland have remained fairly stable since the early 1980s (ISD 1998 1999 2000). However, they look increasingly deviant for a number of reasons. One reason is the fact that almost all teenage births are outside of marriage. There has also been a decline in the birth rate among women in their twenties without an equivalent increase in the abortion rate, making the lack of a similar decline in pregnancy among teenagers more troublesome. Finally, rates of teenage pregnancy and birth have fallen in other European countries leaving the UK at the top of some league tables, although rates of teenage birth remain higher in the USA and New Zealand (Coleman and Chandola 1999).

We now turn to explore attitudes to cohabitation and teenage pregnancy in Scotland and England. To what extent are the differences that have been identified in terms of demographic trends north and south of the border translated into different attitudes? Is the slightly higher rate of marriage and lower rate of cohabitation in Scotland associated with less tolerance of cohabitation? Does the slightly higher rate of teenage births outside of marriage in Scotland mean that people are more or less tolerant of teenage pregnancy? This chapter begins by exploring such attitudes in Scotland and England and highlighting areas where views differ.

Given that both cohabitation and teenage pregnancy are associated with divergence from conventional marriage and parenting, it might be expected that people will hold a coherent set of views around cohabitation, marriage, parenting, and teenage pregnancy. It certainly can be expected that attitudes towards marriage and cohabitation will be related to one another, with certain types of people holding certain 'packages' of views. Likewise, with teenage pregnancy, it would seem probable that certain views are themselves inter-related, and that different groups of the population would hold particular packages of views. This chapter moves on to consider whether this is in fact the case. Are there 'sets' of views on cohabitation and marriage and on teenage pregnancy? Are views divided by age, sex or other characteristics? Does tolerance or condemnation of cohabitation go hand in hand with understanding or condemnation of teenage pregnancy?

If this is the case, it should be relatively easy to predict the types of policy that will be most popular and who they will appeal to most and least. If it is not true, the situation for policy-makers will be less predictable.

ATTITUDES TO COHABITATION

In 2000 the Scottish Social Attitudes Survey explored attitudes to various aspects of the practice of living together as a couple outside of the institution of marriage. A set of questions explored whether respondents believe that unmarried couples should have the same legal rights as married couples. Other questions investigated the moral acceptability to respondents of people living outside of marriage. Some questions explored the respondents' views of the relative merits of marriage and unmarried cohabitation, and of married couples versus cohabitees as parents.

Questions aimed at directly tapping how comfortable people were with the 'rightness' or morality of cohabitation resulted in majority support for cohabitation but with considerable variation by age (Table 3.1). Moral disapproval of cohabitation was higher at older ages. While 86 per cent of 18-24 year olds agreed that it is alright for a couple to live together without intending to get married, majority agreement was not achieved among the over 60s and only 32 per cent of over 65 year olds agreed. Considering the idea of cohabiting to 'test' a marriage, the majority of people thought it a good idea for a couple who intend to get married to live together first; again support was highest among the young. The percentages of residents in England agreeing with these items were very similar to those in Scotland.

Questions inviting a ranking of marriage and cohabitation resulted in the majority favouring marriage, again with notable variation by age (Table 3.2). Over the whole sample, only 16 per cent disagreed that even though it might not work out for some people, marriage is still the best kind of relationship and 61 per cent agreed. Agreement with this statement ranged from 87 per cent of those aged over 65 to 31 per cent among 18-24 year olds, many of whom remained neutral or undecided. Most young people did not agree with the characterisation of those who cohabit as being scared of the commitment of marriage, a view only widely endorsed by older respondents. Even among the youngest group, only a small minority of respondents agreed that 'there is no point in getting married – it's only a piece of paper': 19 per cent of 18-24 year olds agreed in comparison with nine per cent of the over 65 year old age group. But all age groups were inclined to endorse the view that 'too many people just drift into marriage without thinking about it'. Overall agreement in England was almost identical to that in Scotland on all of these items.

Table 3.1 Percentage of people agreeing with 'rightness' or morality of cohabitation

	Scotland			England
	Aged 18-24	Aged 65+	All	All
It is alright for a couple to live together without intending to get married	86	32	66	67
It is a good idea for a couple who intend to get married to live together first	70	31	55	56
Sample size	132	356	1506	2515

When respondents were asked to choose between the suitability of unmarried cohabitation versus marriage as circumstances for bringing up children, support for marriage remained strong. Overall, 55 per cent agreed that people who want children ought to get married, but again with significant variation by age, ranging from 86 per cent among the over 65 year olds to 31 per cent among 18-24 year olds, among whom 43 per cent disagreed. Fewer respondents were prepared to go as far as agreeing that married couples make better parents than unmarried ones, a view with which only 26 per cent of the whole sample agreed and 40 per cent disagreed. Again the pattern was very similar in England. This is a question on which there was some variation between men's and women's answers in Scotland, with women less likely than men to agree (Table 3.3).

Table 3.2 Percentage of people agreeing with statements about marriage and cohabitation

	Scotland			England
	18-24	65+	All	All
Even though it might not work out for some people, marriage is still the best kind of relationship	32	87	61	59
Many people who live together without getting married are just scared of the commitment	22	56	35	36
Too many people just drift into marriage without really thinking about it	60	77	69	69
People who want children ought to get married	31	86	55	54
Sample size	132	356	1506	2515

Table 3.3 Percentage of men and women of different ages agreeing 'Married couples make better parents than unmarried ones'

	Men			Women		
	18-24	25-34	65+	18-24	25-34	65+
	24	13	62	7	7	49
Sample size	53	125	133	79	143	223

Young men aged 18-24 were surprisingly conservative with respect to the question of whether married couples make better parents than unmarried one. Twenty-four per cent agreed that married couples make better parents in comparison to only 13 per cent of 25-34 year old men and only 7 per cent of 18-34 year old women. For women and for men aged over 25, agreement that married couples make better parents increased with age.

The pattern of age and sex variation was broadly similar in England, but young men in England were even more likely to take a conservative stance than those in Scotland (27 per cent of those aged 18-24 years and 21 per cent of 25-34 year old men agreed that married couples make better parents). Older people in England were slightly less likely to agree that married couples make better parents than their Scottish counterparts.

So, in general, we found the Scottish public demonstrating considerable acceptance of cohabitation although it did not have quite such approved of status as marriage, particularly among older people. The majority of people were in favour of cohabitation to 'test' a marriage. Views on cohabitation in Scotland were not notably different from those in England.

ATTITUDES TOWARDS TEENAGE PREGNANCY

People in Scotland were strongly of the view that levels of teenage pregnancy are problematic in Britain, with only seven per cent saying that teenage pregnancy isn't really much of a problem (Table 3.4). Given the wide prevalence of this view, it is interesting that half of those surveyed thought that people in Britain were too tolerant of teenage pregnancy. Perhaps people do not believe that most people share their views, or perhaps they feel that there is not enough being done to tackle the problem. While most people believed that teenage pregnancy is a problem, half the population took the view that a teenager can be just as good a parent as someone older, and half disagreed. Concern for the children of teenage mothers is therefore likely to be one aspect of people's disapproval of teenage pregnancy. Another concern may be for the mothers themselves. Almost three quarters of people thought that teenage girls who want to get on in life do not usually become teenage mothers.

Compared with people in Scotland, those in England were significantly more negative in their attitudes to teenage parenting. Only 38 per cent of those in England felt teenagers could be as good parents as older people (compared with 50 per cent in Scotland holding this view).

Table 3.4 Percentage of people agreeing with general views on teenage pregnancy

	Scotland	England
Teenage girls who want to get on in life don't usually become teenage mothers	73	72
A teenager can be just as good a parent as someone who is older	50	38
People in Britain are far too tolerant of teenage pregnancies	49	55
Teenage pregnancy isn't really that much of a problem in Britain	7	5
Sample size	1506	2515

We now turn to look at people's attitudes towards teenage pregnancy in relation to single-parenthood (Table 3.5). Here we see that the vast majority of people felt that bringing up a child alone is too hard for most teenage girls (80 per cent). Far fewer people shared this concern if the mother in question was not a teenager. Under half the population (41 per cent) believed single parenthood in general to be too hard for a woman. Whether most people believe that teenage mothers are single or in stable relationships, we also found that negative views of teenage pregnancy extended to teenage couples in a stable relationship. Only a quarter of people thought there was nothing wrong with a couple aged 16 or over and in a stable relationship having a child. In light of this finding and the fact (reported above) that half of those interviewed thought a teenager could be as good a parent as someone older, it seems that more people are concerned that teenagers themselves, rather than their children, suffer as a consequence of teenage parenting.

Respondents in England were even more likely than those in Scotland to take the view that bringing up a child is too hard for teenage girls to do alone (84 compared with 80 per cent). Fewer of those in England thought it was all right for a teenage couple in a stable relationship to have a baby (18 compared with 26 per cent in Scotland held this view).

**Table 3.5 Percentage agreeing with attitudes towards teenage pregnancy
and lone parenthood**

	Scotland	England
Bringing up a child is simply too hard for most teenage girls to do alone	80	84
Bringing up a child is simply too hard for a woman of any age to do alone	41	41
If a teenage couple aged 16 or older are in a stable relationship there is nothing wrong with them having a child	26	18
Sample size	1506	2515

With such strong censorship of teenage pregnancy, it is interesting now to look at views on the causes of teenage pregnancy and the possible solutions to this problem (Table 3.6).

There was certainly a view that societal factors outside the control of teenagers play a role. Six in ten people believed that television and advertising put teenagers under too much pressure to have sex before they are ready and the same proportion believed that teenage girls in run down areas are more likely than others to become teenage mothers. Half the population thought that Britain's welfare system often rewards teenage mothers and a slightly smaller proportion took the view that teenage girls who have children often do so to jump the housing queue. A lack of morals among young people was said by half (52 per cent) to be one of the main causes of teenage pregnancy. Just under one in three people felt that teenage mothers have babies because they want someone to love.

Respondents in England were more likely to feel that Britain's welfare system rewards teenage mothers than those in Scotland (56 compared with 49 per cent). Those in England also appeared more likely to see a lack of morals among young people as a cause of teenage pregnancy although this difference was not statistically significant.

Table 3.6 Percentage agreeing with various views on the causes of teenage pregnancy

	Scotland	England
Television and advertising put teenagers under too much pressure to have sex before they are ready	61	62
Teenage girls living in run down areas are more likely than others to become teenage mothers	59	62
One of the main causes of teenage pregnancy is the lack of morals among young people	52	56
All too often Britain's welfare system rewards teenage mothers	49	56
Teenage girls who have children often do so to jump the housing queue	43	46
Many teenage mothers simply have babies because they want someone to love	29	27
Sample size	1506	2515

Given high levels of concern about teenage pregnancy it is perhaps not surprising that many people saw benefits in the various ways to reduce teenage pregnancy suggested – even though some of them might be expected to be highly contentious (Table 3.7). Almost three quarters of those surveyed felt that there would be fewer teenage pregnancies if more parents talked to their children about sex, relationships and contraception. A somewhat smaller proportion (although still a majority of the population at 56 per cent) thought that teenage pregnancies would be reduced if sex education at school gave advice about these topics. Over six in ten people thought that contraception should be more easily available to teenagers, even if they are under 16. In fact, GPs and contraceptive clinics can legally provide contraception to those under 16 but this may not be widely known. It is sometimes suggested that sex education can actually encourage children to have sex too early. This view was held by just 22 per cent of those surveyed. Reducing teenage pregnancies through abortions was not a popular idea. Just 15 per cent of people felt that pregnant teenagers should be encouraged to consider having an abortion. This question was potentially ambiguous – people may have understood it to mean that abortion should be one of the options presented to pregnant teenage girls, or they may have understood it to mean that such girls should be encouraged to have an abortion.

Views on these issues did not vary between Scotland and England, with the exception of a higher proportion of English respondents favouring abortions for teenage mothers (21 compared with 15 per cent). It is difficult to interpret this difference in light of the different possible understandings of the question.

Views of teenage pregnancy have been found to be generally negative as people feel it reduces opportunities for the parents if not causing harm to the children. The Scottish public is slightly less authoritarian in views of teenage pregnancy than the public in England.

Table 3.7 Percentage agreeing with various solutions to teenage pregnancy by age

	Scotland	England
There would be fewer teenage pregnancies if parents talked to their children about sex, relationships and contraception	73	74
Contraception should be more easily available to teenagers, even if they are under 16	62	65
There would be fewer teenage pregnancies if sex education at school gave more advice about sex, relationships and contraception	56	55
Giving teenagers lessons at school about sex and contraception encourages them to have sex too early	22	22
Pregnant teenagers should be encouraged to consider having an abortion	15	21
Sample size	1506	2515

INTER-RELATIONSHIPS BETWEEN VIEWS

Having examined, at a broad level, the views of the Scottish population with regard to matters of marriage, cohabitation and teenage pregnancy, we now turn to consider which of the opinions are themselves inter-related and then examine whether certain groups of the population are particularly likely to hold certain views.

Factor analysis was used to identify groupings of items for which respondents tended to hold similar views. (Factor analysis is described in the Appendix to the book.) All the marriage, cohabitation and teenage pregnancy attitude variables discussed above were included in the analysis. Two sets of variables were combined to form scales as a result of this analysis.

Seven items pertaining to marriage and cohabitation emerged as related and were used to form a scale showing the extent to which people believe marriage is superior to cohabiting. The items in this scale[2] were:

It is all right for a couple to live together without intending to get married.

It is a good idea for a couple who intend to get married to live together first.

There is no point getting married – it's only a piece of paper.

People who want children ought to get married.

Married couples make better parents than unmarried ones.

Even though it might not work out for some people, marriage is still the best kind of relationship.

Many people who live together without getting married are just scared of the commitment.

One of the marriage variables reported on earlier was not included in this scale: 'Too many people just drift into marriage without really thinking about it'.

The second set of views to emerge related to teenage pregnancy. This brought together the following five items and created a scale showing the extent to which people hold authoritarian views of teenage pregnancy:[3]

Teenage girls who have children often do so to jump the housing queue.

All too often Britain's welfare system rewards teenage mothers.

People in Britain are far too tolerant of teenage pregnancies.

One of the main causes of teenage pregnancy is the lack of morals among young people.

Giving teenagers lessons in school about sex and contraception encourages them to have sex too early.

The factor analysis suggested that there were also relationships between some of the other teenage pregnancy variables, but scales created as a result were found to have weak reliability and so were not used.

The variables brought together in the factor analysis suggested that there was some correlation between the following measures concerning causes of and solutions to teenage pregnancy:

There would be fewer teenage pregnancies if more parents talked to their children about sex, relationships and contraception.

There would be fewer teenage pregnancies if sex education at school gave more advice about sex, relationships and contraception.

Contraception should be more easily available to teenagers, even if they are under 16.

Teenage girls living in run down areas are more likely than others to become teenage mums.

Television and advertising put teenagers under too much pressure to have sex before they are ready.

It also appeared from the factor analysis that three variables suggesting that teenage pregnancy is 'not a problem' were related:

If a teenage couple aged 16 or older are in a stable relationship there is nothing wrong with them having a child.

Teenage pregnancy isn't really that much of a problem in Britain.

A teenager can be just as good a parent as someone who is older.

Variables that did not appear in any of the clusters above were the view that many teenage mothers simply have babies because they want somebody to love, the view that pregnant teenagers should be encouraged to have an abortion, and the two measures considering views on bringing up a child being too hard for teenage girls, and then for women of any age, to do alone. The factor analysis thus suggests that while there is something of a 'package' of views that people hold on marriage and cohabitation, views on teenage pregnancy are more varied. Beyond the one set of views which consider the rightness or wrongness of teenagers becoming parents, respondents may hold many combinations of attitudes.

In subsequent analysis we consider the two scales on marriage and cohabitation and on authoritarian views towards teenage pregnancy rather than consider the variables that make up these scales independently. We then consider individual variables reflecting other aspects of people's attitudes towards teenage pregnancy – taking some variables reflecting the 'causes and solutions' dimension to teenage pregnancy and some variables relating to the view that teenage pregnancy is 'not a problem'. First we outline the way in which the scales were created.

For the scale showing confidence in marriage, four of the items required people to agree in order to show confidence while the remaining three required people to disagree in order to show confidence. These latter three scales were reversed so that a score of 1 represented strong agreement with the statement in question and a score of 5 showed strong disagreement. Respondents' total scores across the seven items were than calculated giving a possible range between 7 and 35. Total scores were then divided by 7 to give values between 1 and 5, and respondents were allocated to one of three roughly equal-sized groups: the most pro-marriage group (those who scored 1 to 2.58), the middle group (who scored 2.7 to 3.15) and the least pro-marriage group (who scored 3.28 to 5.0). The first of these groups can be said to have strong confidence in the superiority of marriage over cohabitation, while the middle group had less confidence about this and the third group had very little or no confidence in the superiority of marriage over cohabitation.

A similar scale was created for the scale showing the extent of authoritarianism that respondents displayed with regard to teenage pregnancy. For each of the five items in the scale a score of 1 (strongly agree) to 5 (strongly disagree) was possible. Summing respondents' scores gave values ranging from 5 to 25, which were then divided by 5 to give values between 1 and 5. Depending on their scores, respondents were allocated to one of three groups: most authoritarian third (scores of 1 to 2.4), middle third (scores of 2.6 to 3.1), and least authoritarian third (scores of 3.2 to 5).

Table 3.8 shows that around one third of people did fall into each of the three categories on the two measures in Scotland. Using the same classifications for England, we found levels of confidence in marriage to be very similar in the two countries, while more people in England were in the most authoritarian group in terms of views on teenage pregnancy (40 compared with 35 per cent in Scotland). This is interesting in light of the trends in the two countries – marriage rates being slightly higher in Scotland and teenage pregnancies outside of marriage being lower in England. Scotland has a higher marriage rate but no more public support for marriage, and, alongside a higher rate of teenage births outside marriage, less condemnation of teenage pregnancy.

One clear display of the fact that views did not overlap substantially outside of these two scales is demonstrated in the following table, which relates the two scales to one another for Scotland. It can be seen that one in five people were both confident in the superiority of marriage and authoritarian in their views on teenage pregnancy. At the other end of the scale one in five were not pro-marriage and were least authoritarian in their views of teenage pregnancy. Six in ten people lay between these two extremes, with between four per cent and 11 per cent in each of seven cells denoting different positions. While it is not possible to pigeonhole the population into two definite clusters of views, it is the case that those who are most authoritarian on teenage pregnancy are also more likely to be very pro-marriage than not and those who are least authoritarian in this respect are also less likely to be pro-marriage.

Table 3.8 Scales showing degree of confidence in marriage and level of authoritarianism in views on teenage pregnancy

	Scotland	England
Degree of confidence in marriage as superior to cohabitation		
Most confident in the superiority of marriage over cohabitation	33	34
Middle	33	31
Least confident in the superiority of marriage over cohabitation	35	35
Degree of authoritarianism in relation to teenage pregnancy		
Most authoritarian	35	40
Middle	30	31
Least authoritarian	35	29
Sample size	1523	2515

Table 3.9 Percentage of people holding each pair of views on the teenage pregnancy and marriage/cohabitation scales

	Extent of authoritarianism in relation to teenage pregnancy		
Degree of pro-marriage feeling	Most	Middle	Least
Very pro-marriage	19	10	4
Middle	11	11	11
Not or a little pro-marriage	4	10	20

Sample size=1506, Cells sum to 100%

Aside from some consideration of attitudes towards marriage and cohabitation in relation to age and sex, thus far we have not considered the extent to which different sections of society may differ in their views. We now turn to examine the effects on attitudes of factors such as age, level of education, sex, religion and religious attendance, social class, political party identification, newspaper readership, main source of income, tenure, marital status, and whether the respondent had a child while they were a teenager, later, or not at all ('parental status'). Multiple regression analysis was undertaken to identify which of these characteristics had a significant independent relationship with the marriage and teenage pregnancy scales. Logistic regression analysis was used to consider those characteristics with a significant independent relationship with five additional views related to teenage pregnancy. More information on these techniques is found in the Appendix to the book. In the remaining tables in this chapter, variables are presented only if they emerged as having a significant effect, independent of other variables, in the regression models. Thus there may be other factors for which relationships with attitudes to marriage and cohabitation, and teenage pregnancy, would be significant, but these relationships did not remain once other variables in the model had been taken into consideration.

Firstly, who holds the view that marriage is superior to cohabitation and who is less confident in the superiority of marriage? Factors that emerged as significant from the model were age, religious attachment, marital status, political party identification, daily newspaper readership, main source of income, and parental status.

Support for marriage as superior to cohabitation has already been shown to be much more common among older people: seven in ten of those aged 65 and over were in the most pro-marriage group compared with only one in ten of those aged 18-34.

Unsurprisingly, the marital status of respondents was related to their views on marriage and cohabitation. While seven in ten widows and four in ten of those currently married were in the most pro-marriage group, only two in ten of those divorced or separated were in this group – and only two in a hundred co-habitees were. The loss of faith in marriage among those who were divorced or separated was no greater than the lack of confidence in marriage among the single, never married respondents – just over half of both groups were in the least pro-marriage group. Seven in ten co-habitees were in the least pro-marriage group.

If marital status signifies personal histories that influence people's views, so too does whether or not people have children and the age at which they became parents. Six in ten of those who became parents as teenagers, regardless of their age now, were in the least pro-marriage group – only one in ten were in the most pro-marriage group. This is perhaps not surprising, because teenage births are often outside of marriage, and because, when couples marry and have children young, their marriages are particularly susceptible to breakdown. Parents who had their children later had relatively high membership of the most pro-marriage group, in line with the widespread view that marriage is better for children (41 per cent were in this group). Those with no children were more likely to be in the least pro-marriage group than in the group most supportive of marriage (46 compared with 21 per cent).

It might be expected that religious devotion would be associated with more conservative views about such issues as marriage versus cohabitation – and there is clear evidence that this is the case, although the type of religion is also significant (Table 3.10). Members of the Church of Scotland who attended church at least once a month were found to be least supportive of cohabitation. Church of Scotland members who attended church less frequently had similar views to Catholics who attended church at least once a month. These groups were less supportive of cohabitation than those of no religion or Catholics who attended church less than once a month.

Given the different ideologies of the various political parties in Scotland, it is not surprising that identification with particular parties was also related to membership of the most pro-marriage and the least pro-marriage groups. Over half of those who identified with the Conservative party (53 per cent) were in the most pro-marriage group while only a quarter of Liberal Democrat and SNP supporters were in this group. Just under a third (31 per cent) of Labour supporters were in the most pro-marriage group.

People's choice of daily newspaper was also related to their views on marriage and cohabitation. Those who read no newspaper, the Scottish *Sun* and minority choices listed under 'other' (predominantly broadsheets published in London) were more likely than readers of other papers to fall into the group who were least pro-marriage – around four in ten did so. Around half of those who read the *Herald, Mail, Express, Press and Journal*, or *Dundee Courier* were in the most pro-marriage group.

Table 3.10 Membership of most and least pro-marriage groups, by religious status

Religion and religiosity	Most pro-marriage	Least pro-marriage	Sample size
Church of Scotland – attends church at least monthly	62	13	185
Church of Scotland – attends less frequently	41	23	357
Catholic – attends church at least monthly	46	26	95
Catholic –attends less frequently	20	41	81
Other Christian or other religion	44	24	181
No religion	17	50	607
All respondents	33	35	1506

Finally, and perhaps more surprisingly, respondents' main source of income was related to these attitudes. This was largely due to the fact that two thirds of those for whom income support or unemployment benefit was the main source of income were in the least pro-marriage group. Those for whom pensions were the main source of income were most likely to be in the most pro-marriage group, but this is explained by age, which we have already considered.

We now turn to look at the second scale we created, showing how authoritarian people's views of teenage pregnancy were. Here we find that all of the characteristics identified as being related to views towards marriage and cohabitation were also relevant in explaining authoritarian attitudes towards teenage pregnancy. In addition, respondents' highest educational qualification also had a bearing (half of those with no qualifications were in the most authoritarian group in their views of teenage pregnancy compared with just 17 per cent of those with university degrees).

In general, the groups who were pro-marriage were most authoritarian in their views of teenage pregnancy. However, often the levels of conviction were not as strong for opinions on teenage pregnancy as for views towards marriage. This may help to explain the fact that the teenage pregnancy scale did not correlate strongly with the marriage and cohabitation scale (as we saw in Table 3.9). It is also possible that in some cases the same kinds of people, rather than the same people, may hold certain views.

The fact that the same variables were significant in the models concerned with attitudes towards teenage pregnancy and marriage and cohabitation, but with groups taking less extreme positions, suggests that people may be less confident in their views on the issue of teenage pregnancy. For example, while membership of the most pro-marriage group ranged from two per cent of cohabitees to 72 per cent of widows, for the issue of teenage pregnancy, 17 of cohabitees and 57 per cent of widows were in the most authoritarian category. Again both these groups represented the extremes of the distribution according to marital status. Likewise 62 per cent of Church of Scotland members who attended church regularly were in the most pro-marriage group and only 53 per cent were in the group who were most authoritarian in their views of teenage pregnancy. Even those who had been teenage parents were more likely to be in the least pro-marriage group (62 per cent) than in the least authoritarian group in terms of views towards teenage pregnancy (55 per cent).

Although it is becoming clear that the idea that there are 'packages' of views held by large groups of the population is too simplistic, relating the scales to one another for different groups shows that, for a few subsets of society, views are more coherent (Table 3.11). Half of those whose main income was a state pension were in the most pro-marriage group and the most authoritarian group in terms of attitudes towards teenage pregnancy. This combination of views was also held by 46 per cent of widows. Forty six per cent of cohabitees and 45 per cent of teenage parents were in both the least pro-marriage group and the least authoritarian groups towards teenage pregnancy.

Having considered the scales, we now look in more detail at some of the individual attitudes towards teenage pregnancy that were not included in the scales. First we consider the views that teenagers can be as good parents as those who are older, and that there is nothing wrong with teenagers aged 16 or over in a stable relationship having a child (Table 3.12). Overall half the respondents in Scotland agreed with the first statement and just one quarter agreed with the second. Nineteen per cent of those interviewed agreed with both statements.

A more common pattern was not to agree with either statement – over four in ten respondents did this.

Table 3.11 Combinations of views towards marriage and towards teenage pregnancy, for selected groups

Sub-group	Most pro-marriage AND most reactionary in views of teenage pregnancy	Least pro-marriage AND least reactionary in views of teenage pregnancy	Sample size
All respondents	19	20	1506
Cohabitee	1	46	105
Teenage parent	6	45	119
Income support/ unemployment benefit as main source of income	6	41	120
Divorced/ separated	8	36	181
Single	8	31	327
Degree level qualification	12	33	202
Not a parent	11	26	430
No qualifications	29	10	488
Conservative	33	5	253
Widow	46	16	213
State pension as main source of income	52	2	283

Cells show the percentage of all people in sub group falling into relevant categories.

Perhaps unsurprisingly, those who had had a child when they were a teenager themselves were particularly likely to agree that teenagers could be as good parents as older parents – almost three quarters of this group held this view. Conservatives and members of the salariat were least likely to agree.

The view that there is nothing wrong with a teenage couple in a stable relationship having a baby was particularly strong among those who had a baby as a teenager – although even among this group a majority did not agree (45 per cent). Those who had children at later ages were more likely to oppose teenage births than those who had not had children. Men were more likely than women to take the view that there was nothing wrong with a teenage couple in a stable relationship having a baby (31 compared with 28 per cent held this view). It is not clear whether these differences reflect moral judgements or different appraisals of the practical difficulties involved in teenage parenting. Conservative party supporters, those who were regular churchgoers (whether Church of Scotland or Catholic) and those in the higher social class groups were least likely to agree that there was nothing wrong with these births to teenagers.

While 43 per cent of all respondents disagreed with both statements, among the following groups half or more of respondents disagreed with both views and were thus particularly anti-teenage pregnancy: regular attenders of the Church of Scotland, Conservative identifiers, people aged 65 and over, those in the salariat social class group, and those who had degrees or equivalent qualifications. Groups who held the opposite views most strongly – agreeing with both statements – were those who had themselves been teenage parents (37 per cent), those in the manual foreman or supervisor social class group (30 per cent) and those whose main source of income was income support or unemployment benefit (29 per cent).

We turn now to the view that teenage girls living in rundown areas are more likely than others to become teenage mothers (Table 3.13). There is some factual basis for this statement as teenage pregnancy rates are slightly higher in areas of higher deprivation (McLeod 2001). However, there is no way of knowing whether those who agree with the statement are aware of this fact and share the government's concern with social exclusion and tackling problems on an area basis. It is also possible that negative stereotypes of 'rundown areas' are being invoked. It would seem that this view is most widely shared by the most highly educated members of society. Other significant factors emerging from our regression analysis were sex, parental status, main source of income, and social class.

Table 3.12 Percentage of people in each cell – that is, holding each pair of views

	A teenager can be just as good a parent as someone older		
If a teenage couple aged 16 or over are in a stable relationship, there's nothing wrong with them having a child	Agree	Disagree, or Neither agree nor disagree	All
Agree	19	8	26
Disagree, or Neither agree nor disagree	31	43	74
All	50	50	100

Sample size=1506, Cells sum to 100%

Eighty per cent of those with degrees agreed that teenage pregnancy is more common in rundown areas, compared with just half of those with no qualifications and under 60 per cent of those with qualifications below degree level.

Men were also notably more likely to agree that teenage pregnancy is more prevalent among girls living in rundown areas than women (65 compared with 55 per cent) and those without children were more likely than others to agree with this. Interestingly, those on income support or unemployment benefit, who are perhaps most likely to be living in rundown areas, were least likely to agree with this view (48 per cent did so). It is unclear whether these people were resisting stereotypes of their areas, or speaking from experience. Respondents' housing tenures did not emerge as significant from this model. The proportion of people agreeing with the statement was very similar for owner-occupiers and those in social rented housing.

We turn now to variables suggesting possible solutions to the problem of teenage pregnancy, in particular the views that sex education at school, parents talking to their children more about sex, relationships and contraception, and wider availability of contraception for teenagers might reduce levels of teenage pregnancy. All of these solutions had majority support in the population. We now consider variations between different groups in society.

Table 3.13 Teenage girls living in run down areas are more likely than others to become teenage mothers

Highest educational qualification	% agreeing	Sample size
Degree	80	202
Higher grades and / or other higher education below degree	58	410
Standard grades 1-7 or equivalent	59	402
No qualifications	51	488
All respondents	59	1506

The view that there would be fewer teenage pregnancies if more parents talked to their children about sex, relationships and contraception was supported by almost three quarters of the population. Interestingly, analysis by age finds that the group least likely to agree with this was the youngest cohort – those aged 18-24 and who would have most recent experience of being in the age group at risk of teenage pregnancies. Sixty four per cent of this group – still a majority – agreed that it would help to reduce teenage pregnancies. It may be that more parents these days do discuss these issues and that, while older people think back to their experience as children, the youngest group does not feel that more discussion is required. Alternatively, it might be that younger people see other solutions as having potentially more impact. Indeed, both the other suggestions offered – more advice in sex education lessons at school, and wider availability of contraception, even to those under 16 – were seen by those in the youngest age cohorts as more valuable than parents talking to them about these issues.

In regression analysis social class was the only variable that was found to have a significant independent effect in explaining differences in agreement with the view that parents should talk to their children more about sex, relationships and contraception. Those in the working class, and whose social class could not be classified, were least likely to agree. An emphasis on the value of 'talk' is perhaps a more middle-class notion whereas 'doing' may be more valued by working class people.

With regard to the view that sex education at school should give more advice on these issues, respondents' age, sex and housing tenure group were found to be significant in explaining differences in attitudes. Two thirds of those aged 18-34 saw benefit in this, compared with around half of those in all other age groups. Men were more likely than women to think that teenage pregnancies would be reduced if schools gave more advice about sex, relationships and contraception (60 compared with 52 per cent). Those who owned their own home were less likely than renters to agree with this – renters who were not in social rented housing (including the small number of people living rent-free) were most likely to agree (70 per cent did so compared with 50 per cent of those who owned their home).

The potentially controversial view that contraception should be more easily available even to teenagers under the age of 16 received support from a majority of the population – over six in ten people. Regression analysis revealed that attitudes were influenced by age, religiosity, marital status, parental status, and the respondent's main source of income. Eight in ten of those aged 18-34 were in favour of making access to contraception easier, a proportion that declined with age – falling to just four in ten of those in the oldest age group, 65+ (Table 3.14).

There was also a strong relationship between religiosity and views on contraception. Over seven in ten of those with no religion agreed it should be more widely available. Among Church of Scotland members who attended church monthly only four in ten agreed that contraception should be more easily available. The corresponding figure for equally frequent Catholic churchgoers was five in ten. Six in ten members of both churches who were less frequent attenders were in favour of easier access to contraception. Other groups who were particularly likely to feel that contraception should be more easily available were those cohabiting with a partner and single people. Easier access to contraception was endorsed as likely to be effective by those who had themselves been a teenage parent – 84 per cent of this group felt that contraception should be more easily available to teenagers. Those on social security benefits – income support, unemployment benefit and disability benefits – were also particularly likely to take this view.

Table 3.14 Contraception should be more easily available to teenagers, even if they are under 16

	% agreeing	Sample size
Age		
18-24	83	132
25-34	79	268
35-44	65	315
45-54	59	232
55-59	51	95
60-64	52	107
65+	43	356
All respondents	62	1506

Table 3.15 Percentage of people in each cell – that is, holding each pair of views

	Contraception should be more easily available to teenagers, even if they are under 16		
There would be fewer teenage pregnancies if sex education at school gave more advice about sex, relationships and contraception	Agree	Disagree, or Neither agree nor disagree	All
Agree	39	16	56
Disagree, or Neither agree nor disagree	23	21	44
All	62	38	100

Sample size=1506, Cells sum to 100%

Looking again for overlap between attitudes, just under 40 per cent of people agreed both that sex education classes in schools should give advice on sex, relationships and contraception, and that contraception should be more easily available, even to those under 16 years old (Table 3.15). Just over one in five people agreed with neither of these suggestions.

Among certain sub-groups of the population, views on these issues were more clear cut. For example, 59 per cent of 18-24 year olds and 54 per cent of 25-34 year olds agreed with both statements, as did almost half (46 per cent) of those with degrees. A third of those aged 65 or over agreed with neither statement. These figures still do not endorse the suggestion that there might be clear 'packages' of views on issues of teenage pregnancy. It really does appear that people hold disparate views on these issues and that although factors such as age, religiosity and education affect opinions, they do not form neat patterns that could be easily predicted. One final illustration of this comes from combining the positions most likely to be taken by young people on a number of issues, namely:

Least pro-marriage.

Least authoritarian in views of teenage pregnancy.

Agreeing neither that teenagers can make as good parents as older parents nor that there is nothing wrong with a teenage couple in a stable relationship aged 16 or older having a child.

Agreeing that there would be fewer teenage pregnancies if sex education classes in schools gave more advice on sex, relationships and contraception and that contraception should be more widely available.

We then find that only 3 per cent of all respondents (a total of 45 people, most of them young) took all of these positions. A similar exercise looking at the positions most likely to be taken by elderly respondents showed exactly the same – three per cent (predominantly elderly) held all the respective views.

CONCLUSION

This chapter has endeavoured to present a picture of attitudes towards both marriage and cohabitation and teenage pregnancy in Scotland. A wide range of variables have been considered in the analysis, and comparisons with the situation in England have been made.

Overall, respondents demonstrated considerable acceptance of cohabitation, but without necessarily placing it on a par with marriage. Support for cohabitation does not seem to amount to a strong rejection of conventional forms of partnering and parenting. At the same time, definite confidence in the superiority of marriage was not widespread, and even among the elderly large minorities do not agree that married couples make better parents. The general pattern of attitudes to marriage and cohabitation in Scotland was similar to that in England.

People in both Scotland and England were strongly opposed to teenage pregnancy – even a teenage couple in a stable relationship having a baby – and believed this to be a problematic issue. While this could be read as support for more traditional family building, it seems to be the combination of youth and the burdens of parenthood that are seen as troublesome rather than deviation from conventional patterns of marriage and parenting. Concern about teenage parenting is far more widespread than general concern about lone parenting, and half of people in Scotland acknowledge that teenagers can be good parents. A scale created to show levels of authoritarianism in views towards teenage pregnancy placed more people in England in the most authoritarian group.

Many of the attitudes considered vary notably by factors such as age, educational qualifications, religious affiliation and political party identification. There were also notable relationships with experiential factors, such as being a teenage parent, living on income support and marital status.

Age had the most consistent effect on attitudes to cohabitation, and was also important in explaining attitudes to many aspects of teenage pregnancy – particularly views on ways to reduce teenage pregnancy levels. On most measures, the age gradient revealed growing disapproval of cohabitation and teenage pregnancy with age. In terms of views on what might reduce levels of teenage pregnancy, those in the youngest age cohorts, who perhaps offer the most relevant views, were more supportive than their older counterparts of widening availability of contraception and of increasing the role of sex education in schools.

Predicting future attitudes requires deciding whether age differences reflect permanent shifts that will encompass the whole population as the young replace the old or whether there is a cycle in which views change as people become older and have different experiences. Previous British Social Attitudes Surveys have found evidence to suggest that the more liberal views of young people on moral issues will not change as they get older. These differences reflect a shift in attitudes across historical time reflected in differences between generations rather than views that will change with maturation (Park 2000).

It appears that tolerance of cohabitation is likely to grow over time and will encompass larger sections of the population. This does not necessarily mean that support for cohabitation will extend to such an extent that people no longer use it as a stepping stone on the route to marriage. The view that a lack of morals among young people is a major cause of teenage pregnancy varied notably by age, and here again it would appear likely that, over time, this view will lose support. On the other hand, the view that contraception should be made more widely available to teenagers, which again is more popular amongst the youngest cohorts, may or may not be sustained as people grow older. Given that this actually has surprisingly high levels of support even among older people, it may well be that this is also not a view people will grow out of in our current society.

Education was found to influence a number of the views considered. In line with many studies, more highly educated people were found to be more liberal in terms of certain attitudes: for example they were less likely to take the view that marriage was superior to cohabitation than the least educated and less likely to be authoritarian in their views on teenage pregnancy. However, it was notable that there were still significant minorities of highly educated people who did fall into the least liberal of these groups.

Scotland is often portrayed as a relatively religious society – for example in comparison with England – and the two main churches in Scotland are seen as having notably different views on certain topics. (See Chapter 5 for a discussion of whether this view of Scotland is accurate.) Self-categorisation as belonging to a Christian religion and regularity of attendance were both associated with confidence in marriage and condemnation of teenage pregnancy. However, perhaps contrary to possible expectations, Catholics tended to be less convinced of the superiority of marriage than members of the Church of Scotland, and less authoritarian in their views on teenage pregnancy. In fact Catholics were more likely than members of the Church of Scotland to favour widening access to contraception for teenagers. Religiosity is becoming increasingly uncommon in Scotland, with the main churches experiencing an ageing of their membership, and with recruitment in decline among young people. Thus the importance of religious differences is likely to diminish over time.

One of the most interesting things to emerge from the analysis is the lack of relationship between people's views towards the different issues considered in the chapter. People's views on marriage and cohabitation have been found to be strongly related, but those on teenage pregnancy do not form neat groupings which would allow us to predict views on one aspect from views to another. It seems that these are personal views, and although they are related to people's personal characteristics, these relationships are not strong and consistent. Given the diversity of attitudes to aspects of teenage pregnancy, it is perhaps unsurprising that there was not a strong relationship between attitudes to marriage and cohabitation, and attitudes to teenage pregnancy.

This chapter has largely involved exploration of attitudes towards issues of marriage, cohabitation and teenage pregnancy at a time of changing family relationships in Scotland. People's views appear to have some implications for policy-makers; policies designed to bolster marriage are unlikely to be fully in line with people's views on cohabitation – particularly young people's views. However, marriage remains a popular institution in Scotland – as in England. Governmental attempts to reduce teenage pregnancy appear to be in line with public opinion, although many people remain of the view that people in Britain are too tolerant of teenage pregnancy. The views of young people on possible solutions to teenage pregnancy may be of particular interest to policy makers, especially since, among the public at large, there is also widespread support for widening access to contraception and increasing the role of sex education.

REFERENCES

Coleman, D. and Chandola T. (1999), 'Britain's place in Europe's population', in S. McRae (ed.), *Changing Britain: Families and Households in the 1990s*, Oxford: Oxford University Press, pp. 37-67.

Ermisch, J. and Francesconi, M. (2000), 'Patterns of household and family formation', in R. Berthoud and J. Gershuny (eds), *Seven Years in the Lives of British Families: Evidence on the dynamics of social change from the British Household Panel Survey*, London: The Policy Press, pp. 215-38.

Ermisch, J. (2000), *Personal relationships and marriage expectations: evidence from the 1998 British Household Panel Study*, Working Paper 2000-27, Colchester: Institute for Social and Economic Research.

Haskey, J. (1999), 'Cohabitational and marital histories of adults in Great Britain', *Population Trends*, 96, pp. 13-23.

Haskey, J. (2001), 'Cohabitation in Great Britain: past, present and future trends – and attitudes', *Population Trends*, 103, pp. 4-25.

Hope, S., Braunholtz, S., Playfair, A., Dudleston, A., Ingram, D., Martin, C., Sawyer, B. (2000), *Scotland's People: Results from the 1999 Scottish Household Survey, Volume 1 Annual Report*, Edinburgh: HMSO.

ISD (1998), *Teenage Pregnancy in Scotland A Fifteen Year Review 1983-1997*, Health Briefing 98/04, Edinburgh: Information and Statistics Division.

ISD (1999), *Teenage Pregnancy in Scotland 1989-1999*, Health Briefing 99/04, Edinburgh: Information and Statistics Division.

ISD (2000), *Teenage Pregnancy in Scotland 1990-1999*, Health Briefing 00/08, Edinburgh: Information and Statistics Division.

ISD (2000), *Abortion Act Statistics Scotland*, Edinburgh: Information and Statistics Division.

Kiernan, K. (1999), 'Cohabitation in Western Europe', *Population Trends*, 96, pp. 25-32.

McLeod, A. (2001), 'Changing Patterns of Teenage Pregnancy: population based study of small areas', *British Medical Journal*, 323, pp. 199-203.

Morgan, P. (1995), *Farewell to the Family?: Public Policy and Family Breakdown in Britain and the US*, London: Institute for Economic Affairs.

Park, A. (2000), 'The generation game', in R. Jowell, J. Curtice, A. Park, K. Tomson, R. Jarvis, C. Bromley, N. Stanford, *British Social Attitudes: The 17th Report: Focusing on Diversity*, London: Sage, pp. 1-22.

Shaw, C. and Haskey J. (1999), 'New estimates and projections of the population cohabiting in England and Wales', *Population Trends*, 95, pp. 7-17.

---

[1] GHS data were obtained from the ESRC Data Archive at the University of Essex for this analysis.

[2] Cronbach's alpha measure of reliability for the marriage/ cohabitation scale was 0.825, a high level.

[3] Cronbach's alpha measure of reliability for the teenage pregnancy scale was 0.784, a high level.

4

COHABITATION AND MARRIAGE IN SCOTLAND: ATTITUDES, MYTHS AND THE LAW

ANNE BARLOW

INTRODUCTION

As Family Law is a devolved matter in Scotland, it now falls to the Scottish Executive to consider family policy and legal reform in the light of the changing social trends that are reshaping family structures in Scotland as elsewhere in Britain.

That these social trends are changing is beyond dispute. As already demonstrated in Chapter 3, throughout Britain fewer people are choosing to marry, more are choosing to cohabit and have children outside marriage, often in cohabiting relationships. These trends are clearly echoed in Scotland, although both the decline in marriage and rise in cohabitation here has to date been less steep than in England (see Chapter 3). Furthermore, divorce continues to be high in Scotland with over 1200 divorce actions being filed in 1999 as compared with 850 in 1979 (Scottish Executive 2000: Annex B), again signifying a move away from traditional families based on lifelong marriage partnerships. Despite these trends away from the traditional married family being a little less marked in Scotland than England, the Scottish Executive, in contrast to Westminster, has not only recognised that change in family structuring has taken place but has set out proposals for legal reform which acknowledge this (Scottish Executive 2000). For although as demonstrated in Chapter

3, cohabitation has become a socially acceptable family type and one predicted to double by 2021 (Shaw and Haskey 2000), Family Law in Britain generally and in Scotland in particular is still 'marriage-centric'. This means that the protective nature of Family Law which, for example, redresses economic disadvantage suffered as a result of contributing to a marriage when the marriage ends in breakdown or death, does not extend to cohabiting relationships, however marriage-like they may have been. It is the form rather than the function of the relationship at which the law currently looks. Thus there may be a gap between what people expect family law to do and how it actually treats cohabitants as compared with married couples. Given the Scottish Executive is proposing Family Law reform, it is a poignant time not only to explore current social and moral attitudes to marriage and cohabitation (as has been done in Chapter 3), but also to assess people's awareness (or indeed lack of it) of the contrasting legal positions of married and cohabiting couples. In addition, the views of people in Scotland on the desirability of legal reform in the light of changing family structures are of particular interest in this climate.

Thus in contrast to Chapter 3, this chapter will focus on people's attitudes to marriage and cohabitation as legal (rather than moral or social) institutions. It will consider them against the background of the moral and social attitudes discussed in the last chapter and compare them with findings on these issues in England and Wales. In particular, and using further data from the Scottish Social Attitudes Survey 2000, it will explore people's understanding of the legal implications of different family partnerships and their views on how appropriate these remain in the New Scotland. First, however, a profile of characteristics of those who cohabit rather than marry will be drawn. Are they younger, less religious or politically more radical than their married counterparts? Do they have more or fewer educational qualifications than married folk? Is their any significant variation in social class? Are they more likely to rent or but their home? How does the profile of Scottish cohabitants vary from that of their English counterparts?

COHABITATION AND MARRIAGE IN SCOTLAND – WHO COHABITS AND WHY?

Of the total Scottish survey sample, only seven per cent were currently cohabiting, yet nearly a third (31 per cent) had experienced cohabitation. This was slightly lower than the 35 per cent of those surveyed in England and Wales as part of the British Social Attitudes Survey 2000 who had cohabited. Forty four per cent of the Scottish sample were married and of these 22 per cent had cohabited in the past. In addition, just under half (47 per cent) of those who had ever cohabited had gone on to marry that partner, slightly lower than the 54 per cent in England and Wales. Taken together, this indicates that in Scotland, as in England and Wales, cohabitation is often a prelude to marriage. Indeed, given that the younger the respondent, the more likely they are to have cohabited before marrying, – over half (51 per cent) of those married and under 35 and all of those married and under 25 (a very small group) had cohabited prior to marriage – indications are that pre-marital cohabitation is fast establishing itself as a social norm. Thus clearly a significant number of cohabitation relationships are trial marriages which end in matrimony.

Conversely, does a bad experience of marriage in an earlier relationship lead to a preference to cohabit rather than marry again? Here we found that of the respondents who are currently cohabiting over a quarter (28 per cent) had been married in the past and that this was somewhat lower than the 34 per cent in England and Wales. However, it is not possible to ascertain from the data whether a cohabitant's partner had been previously married. Thus this is the minimum number of cohabiting relationships chosen against a background of a failed previous marriage. Nonetheless, in Scotland, almost three quarters of those cohabiting (72 per cent) had never been married, indicating that for a majority cohabitation is either a positive life-style choice or trial marriage.

COHABITATION AND RELIGION

Interestingly of those who had married and regarded themselves as religious, the proportion who had previously cohabited did not vary with age, but remained constant at 25 per cent. Generally, however, whether or not you regard yourself as religious is a powerful factor in the decision to cohabit or marry. For in Scotland 64 per cent of those who were married considered themselves as having a religion, with 36 per cent holding no religion. Amongst current cohabitants, however, this position was reversed, with 60 per cent having no religion and only 40 per cent classifying themselves as religious. Given that the decline in religious beliefs is a more established trend in England and Wales (see Chapter 5), the no-religion factor may also explain the slightly higher rates of cohabitation there compared with Scotland. However, the same proportion of both the Scottish and English cohabitant samples claimed to have no religion. Certainly it seems, the decline in adherence to religious beliefs, at its sharpest amongst the young, has contributed to both the social acceptability of and the increase in living together outside marriage.

COHABITATION, AGE AND EDUCATION

Another at first sight more surprising factor was the correlation between higher educational qualifications and cohabitation. Generally speaking, cohabitants were far more likely to hold educational qualifications than married couples in Scotland at all levels and married couples were far more likely to have no educational qualifications at all (see Table 4.2). However, once the age differential between married and cohabiting couples (see Table 4.1) is taken into account, the educational achievements of the two groups become almost identical. For 63 per cent of the cohabitants are under 35 as opposed to just 15 per cent of married respondents. The largest group of married respondents – 49 per cent – were aged 35-54, as compared with 34 per cent of cohabitants in this age range. Similarly, just four per cent of cohabitants are over 60, whereas almost seven times this number (27 per cent) in this age group are married.

Table 4.1 Percentage of married and cohabiting respondents by age

	Married	Cohabiting
18-24	0	19
25-34	15	44
35-44	25	21
45-54	24	13
55-59	9	1
60-64	9	1
65 +	18	3
Sample size	732	112

Generally speaking, the younger generation have been exposed to far greater educational opportunities and thus are more likely to have gained educational qualifications. Given that cohabitants are on average far younger than their married counterparts, do these differences disappear when cohabitants and married couples within the same age ranges are compared?

Table 4.2 Percentage of married and cohabiting respondents by highest educational achievement

	Married	Cohabiting
Degree	15	13
Other higher education qualification	17	20
A Level or equivalent	10	16
GCSE or equivalent	25	30
No qualification	33	20
Sample size	732	112

When comparing the married group under 60 with cohabitants in the same age range, the differences in educational achievements become much more marginal and when the over 55 age ranges are eliminated, any distinction between the educational achievements of married and cohabiting respondents virtually disappears in all age groups. What is striking, however, is the similarity in the educational profile of the two groups as can be seen from the example of the 35-44 age group in Table 4.3 below.

Age, like religion, is then an important indicator of the likelihood of cohabitation, with cohabitation being at its most popular with the 25-34 age group. Having allowed for age, however, there appear to be no significant differences in the educational qualifications of the two groups and thus the level of a person's educational achievements does not provide an indicator of whether they are more or less likely to marry rather than cohabit. How then does this tie in with the issue of social class?

Table 4.3 Percentage of married and cohabiting respondents aged 35-44 by highest educational achievement

	Married	Cohabiting
Degree	20	21
Other higher education qualification	20	21
A Level or equivalent	11	24
GCSE or equivalent	28	14
No qualification	20	21
Sample size	181	21

COHABITATION, MARRIAGE AND SOCIAL CLASS

Whilst broadly, cohabiting and married respondents fall into similar socio-economic groups, there is some support for the notion that cohabitants are slightly more concentrated in the lower groups as can be seen from the Table 4.4 below. Cohabitants are less likely to be employers or managers and more likely to be unskilled manual workers or junior non-manual workers than married respondents. However, in the other groups, there is little or no distinction. Neither was there any significant difference between the numbers of married and cohabiting respondents who were unemployed, although slightly more cohabitants fell into this category (Table 4.5). Sixty eight per cent of the cohabiting group and 61 per cent of the married were in paid employment, with with 12 per cent in each group permanently looking after the home. Other than the larger number of cohabitants involved in education or training and the larger number of married respondents who were retired – an obvious consequence of the differing age distribution within the two groups – there is again a striking similarity in their profiles.

ATTITUDES TO COHABITATION AND MARRIAGE

Table 4.4 Percentage of married and cohabiting respondents by socio-economic group

	Married	Cohabiting
Professional	5	6
Employers/managers	20	13
Intermediate non-manual	16	18
Junior non-manual	16	18
Skilled manual	20	20
Semi-skilled manual	16	14
Unskilled manual	6	11
Sample size	732	112

Table 4.5 Percentage of married and cohabiting respondents by main economic activity

	Married	Cohabiting
Full-time education/training	0	5
Paid work	61	69
Unemployed	1	4
Permanently sick or disabled	4	5
Retired	20	4
Permanently sick or disabled	4	5
Sample size	732	112

Another related indicator, is housing tenure, but again the position of cohabitants was in line with the trends of the general population. In Scotland, 63 per cent of the whole sample were owner occupiers, slightly lower than the 68 per cent in England and Wales.

In both samples, a clear majority of cohabitants were also owner occupiers, although again this was a lower in Scotland (57 per cent) as compared with England and Wales (65 per cent). However, there is some evidence that, politically, at least, the profiles of cohabitants differ from those of the married. For in this context cohabitants can be seen to be more 'radical', a factor which may incline them towards a less traditional choice of family structure.

COHABITATION AND MARRIAGE AND POLITICAL IDENTIFICATION

Both in Scotland and England, cohabitants are less likely to vote Conservative and are more likely not to identify with any political party (see Table 4.6). Interestingly in Scotland they are also more likely to be Nationalist, whereas the increased support from this group benefits both Labour and Liberal Democrats in England and Wales. Cohabitants are also much more likely to be politically disaffected or perhaps floating voters as significantly more cohabitants than married respondents indicated that they did not identify with any political party. Again, this is to some extent predictable given the age concentration of cohabitants at the younger end, but may also be indicative of a more general rejection of conventional values, which goes hand in hand with an alternative choice of life-style for some cohabitants.

Table 4.6 Percentage of married and cohabiting respondents by political party identification

	Married	Cohabiting
Conservative	20	10
Labour	35	32
Liberal	8	9
SNP	19	25
Green Party	0	1
Other party	1	2
None	10	17
Sample size	732	112

DURABILITY OF COHABITATION

One issue of great importance to family policy makers is the duration of cohabitation relationships. Some research suggests that cohabitation is 'here to stay, but not for long'. This has found the average duration of cohabiting relationships is a mere two to three years, after which time the vast majority of couples either marry or separate (Ermisch and Francesconi 1999: 5). The potential fragility of cohabitation relationships makes them seem inferior to marriages in the eyes of policy makers and some commentators, particularly where child-raising is involved (Home Office 1998, Morgan 2000). Marriages themselves are subject to high breakdown rates in Scotland as elsewhere in the Britain too, and of course it is impossible to say whether the relationship of any couple who cohabit and have a child together would have fared better or worse if they had married. Childbearing within cohabitation relationships is increasingly common and there is evidence to suggest that many cohabitation relationships begin or are contingently prolonged as a result of an unexpected pregnancy (Smart and Stevens 2000). For the same reasons that 'shotgun weddings' were always statistically more fragile than other marriages, contingent cohabitations are likely to be more prone to relationship breakdown than a committed long-term cohabitation relationship. In our sample, the average duration of cohabiting relationships in Scotland was just under six years, in line with the average in England and Wales of just over 6 years (see Table 4.7 below). This is more than double the two to three year period which an earlier British study had calculated using data collected between 1992 and 1995 (Ermisch et al 1999: 5). Again the median duration average we calculated (as opposed to the mean), was three years rather than less than two indicated in the Ermisch study. Our survey also found that nearly one third (30 per cent) of cohabitation relationships had lasted more that five years, as opposed to the less than one fifth found by Ermisch (Ermisch et al 1999: 5)). This may tend to indicate, given that cohabiting relationships are more common among the younger generation, that more cohabiting couples are remaining as they are rather than marrying. This would confirm that we are right to expect not only the incidence of cohabitation to increase as has been predicted (Shaw and Haskey 2000) but also an increase as time goes on in the average duration of such relationships. If this is the case, cohabiting relationships may not be seen as so potentially damaging to children as some currently view them (see e.g. Morgan 2000).

Table 4.7 Percentage of cohabiting relationships by duration, Scotland

Years	1	2	3	4	5	6	7	8	9	10	10+
%	15	18	15	9	8	3	4	3	3	1	19

Sample size: 112

MARRIED AND COHABITING PARENTHOOD

Well over a quarter (28 eight per cent) of the sample who had ever cohabited had had a child whilst cohabiting. Out of the current cohabitants, a considerably higher proportion, 37 per cent, had a child of that relationship. This confirms that the traditional social norm of child-rearing within marriage has lost much of its force and that for many, parenting and cohabitation now go hand in hand. In Chapter 3, we saw that whilst there was great acceptance of cohabitation, there was still strong support for the idea that marriage and parenthood ought to coincide. Fifty five per cent of those surveyed agreed with the statement that if a couple want children they should marry. Yet this leaves a large minority – 43 per cent – who either disagreed or were neutral about this statement. When asked, however, whether married couples made better parents than unmarried couples, only just over a quarter (26 per cent) were prepared to agree. Indeed the largest group were the 40 per cent who disagreed with this statement, on which a further 30 per cent were neutral. This clearly shows that whilst marriage is still recognised as a valuable parenting structure, there is undoubted appreciation of the fact that it is not necessarily the best or most effective. It would seem that unmarried parents, including therefore cohabiting parents, can and do in the majority's view make parents who are as good as or better than married couples. As demonstrated in the last chapter, younger respondents and particularly women were of this view (see Chapter 3). Interestingly, it is the attitudes of women under 25 which appear to have shifted most markedly away from traditional views. Given the critical role of this group in partnering and parenting decisions they may also be the most influential in how family patterns do actually change in the coming years.

ATTITUDES TO MARRIAGE

Do these attitudes mean that marriage itself has lost or is losing its significance as a social institution for many people? We have seen in the last chapter that this is clearly not the case (see Chapter 3). A mere 10 per cent agreed that marriage was 'only a piece of paper' with a most decisive 71 per cent disagreeing. This mirrors exactly the position taken in England and Wales and thus marriage is still valued as a status and an institution in Britain. As has been demonstrated in Chapter 3, the views of those currently cohabiting did, as might be expected, diverge from the mainstream but were less sceptical about the value of marriage than their counterparts in England and Wales. Thus only 18 per cent of current cohabitants in Scotland as opposed to 23 per cent in England and Wales agreed that marriage was only a piece of paper. Forty six per cent of the Scottish cohabiting sample (higher than the 42 per cent south of the border) disagreed. In Scotland more cohabitants (36 per cent) were neutral than in England in Wales (32 per cent). This may point to less outright rejection of the value of marriage in Scotland, but the differences are small. There are signs that marriage as a status and social institution is valued less by the next generation, who will have experienced more parental divorce than older generations whose own parents were likely to have enjoyed or endured life-long marriage partnerships. There was also clear concern that too many people drift into marriage without thinking about it, with 70 per cent agreeing this was the case.

What, if anything, then is seen as the advantage of marriage? Over half (55 per cent) agreed that marriage provided more financial security, although 43 per cent either disagreed or were neutral. Interestingly this was not felt to be the case to the same degree by those in the younger age ranges. Only 39 per cent of women and 36 per cent of men under 25 agreed with this statement, again revealing a shift away from traditional thinking about the benefits of marriage and reflects a picture almost identical to the views found in England and Wales. These views are important in terms of the continued legal privileging of marriage and people's lack of awareness of the implications of this for those who choose not to marry as discussed below.

ATTITUDES TO COHABITATION

What are current attitudes to cohabitation in Scotland? We have seen in Chapter 3 that a clear majority believe that it is acceptable to live together without marrying. However, cohabitation is often depicted as a relationship without the commitment involved in marriage and indeed this is the basis upon which marriage-like legal remedies are denied cohabitants. However, little more than a third (36 per cent) were prepared to agree that many people who live together are just scared of commitment. A third (33 per cent) took the opposite view, disagreeing with the statement whilst 27 per cent neither agreed nor disagreed. Thus here opinion is fairly evenly divided and certainly does not reveal clear public perception of cohabitation as a relationship only for the uncommitted. People's experiences and views of cohabiting couples' commitment are therefore mixed, but perhaps not more so than those of marriage, given the large numbers who agree that marriages are often a product of drift.

Overall, it can be seen that there is still strong support for marriage as an institution or social status, which is still but to a lessening degree associated with financial security and by a minority with good parenting. Yet there is also recognition that many marriages are less than perfect in terms of the relationship between husband and wife and the notion of marriage-drift. Cohabitation is widely accepted both as a prelude to marriage and as an alternative, even where there are children, with little more than a quarter agreeing that married couples make better parents than unmarried ones.

LEGAL ISSUES

Attitudes to marriage and cohabitation are therefore now permissive. Fewer people hold strong views about unmarried cohabitation and indeed unmarried parenting. Fewer people are living in traditional married families, yet the law in Scotland, is still very marriage-centric and only acknowledges that Family Law-based rules are needed to resolve disputes relating to property when marriages breakdown (see Family Law (Scotland) Act 1985). Those who are married will automatically inherit a share of their partner's estate if they die without leaving a will (Succession Law (Scotland) Act 1964). They are entitled to live in the family home belonging to their spouse both during the marriage and on death if there is no will. A spouse is also entitled to apply for the assets acquired during the marriage to be fairly redistributed in the event of divorce (Family Law (Scotland) Act 1985). However, no similar mechanism has yet been provided to deal with parallel disputes arising between those who live together unmarried, whether or not they have children of the relationship. Rather, they are treated as strangers where property is concerned both on relationship breakdown and death of one partner. The owner of any property, or their next of kin in the event of death without a will, takes all. No account can be taken of the contributions a partner may have made to the welfare of the family, by giving up work to care for children, often at one party's (usually the mother's) economic disadvantage. This is also true where efforts have been made by a non-owner partner to decorate the property, or manage and contribute to the household bills to the advantage to the property-owning partner. Even in the rented sector, whilst a cohabitant may well be able to succeed to a rented tenancy should their partner die, they cannot acquire the tenancy (unlike now in England and Wales), other than possibly by agreement, on breakdown of the relationship. In England and Wales, different rules apply, with marriage again being the sole trigger for a family law framework of rights, but many more piecemeal concessions having been made in recent years to cohabitants. Thus cohabitants can apply for discretionary financial provision if their partner dies without leaving a will (Inheritance (Provision for Family and Dependants) Act 1975 as amended by Law Reform (Succession) Act 1995). They can now apply for a rented tenancy (although not an owner-occupied home) to be transferred to them should the relationship break down (Schedule 7, Family Law Act 1996). In property disputes relating to the owner-occupied family home, the English courts, whilst not adopting the Australian doctrine of unjust enrichment, have been prepared in some (and still unpredictable situations) to use the legal device of so-called 'constructive trusts' to assist some cohabitants whose partner owns the family home and to which they have made some direct contribution (see Barlow 1997: 248-276). However, any such approach has been rejected by the Scottish courts (see Bissett-Johnson 1999, Willcock 2000), although the Scottish Law Commission as long ago as 1991 and most recently the Scottish Executive have put forward proposals to ameliorate the legal position of cohabitants.

Nonetheless, as things presently stand, cohabitants need to have made wills and agreements about the shares they hold in property if they wish to achieve a marriage-like outcome if one partner should die or if the relationship should break down. Let us therefore look at how aware cohabitants in Scotland are for the need to do this.

By way of background, the majority of current cohabitants in our sample (57 per cent) own their accommodation, but less than half of them owned their home jointly. Only six per cent of owner-occupier cohabitants had any written agreement about shares of ownership, leaving 94 per cent dependant on pure property law which is reluctant to look behind the legal title. Only 16 per cent of cohabitants had made wills despite the fact that on the death of a cohabitant in Scotland their surviving partner will not inherit anything and will be unable to remain in the home unless a will has been made. Eighty four per cent of them would therefore have no claim on their partner's assets which may or may not be what they intended.

Furthermore, currently unmarried fathers – whether or not they cohabit with the mother – do not gain parental responsibility or rights for their child at birth. This means they have no legal status with regard to the child and no legal authority in decision-making on such issues as consenting to their medical treatment, decisions about their education, religion or nationality. They are still liable however to support their children financially (Child Support Act 1991), but should the child's mother die, an unmarried father has no automatic parental responsibility or rights in respect of his child. Unmarried fathers can gain parental rights and responsibility in both Scotland and England and Wales by entering into a simple but formal Parental Responsibility Agreement with the mother or by obtaining an order of the court (see s4 Children (Scotland) Act 1995). However, the survey revealed that 94 per cent of past and present cohabitants and 95 per cent of those currently cohabiting had no parental responsibility agreement or order. This is even higher than the frightening 90 per cent in England and Wales in this position and reveals that extremely few cohabiting fathers in Britain have a legal relationship with their children.

One possible reason why cohabitants are so remiss at organising their legal affairs could be that because in some areas, such as income-related social security benefits, for example, which many people experience, cohabitants are treated the same as married couples. Here they are allocated a married couple's allowance as opposed to two individual allowances and may mean that they assume they are regarded as married for all purposes.

To try and disentangle people's legal knowledge and views on what the law should be, we first put to them a series of vignettes concerning the position of married and cohabiting couples in different situations. Subsequently we asked them whether they thought that couples living together had a 'common law marriage' which gave them the same legal rights as married couples. The terms 'common law husband' and 'common law wife' are used colloquially in England and Wales to describe a cohabiting partner, (although legally recognised common law marriage was abolished here in 1753) and are certainly understood, if less used, in Scotland. However, the unique Scottish situation, may also provide more room for confusion. For Scotland alone in the UK does still recognise 'marriage by habit and repute', a form of common law marriage which if established will mean a couple is regarded in law as formally married. They would then need to divorce in the normal way according to divorce law if the relationship breaks down, unlike cohabitants. To establish such a marriage, the parties must be free to validly marry and have been cohabiting as husband and wife in Scotland for long enough for a promise of marriage to be inferred. In addition, the couple must be consistently regarded by most other people as married. There is case law on the standard and nature of proof required, although there are only some four to eight cases per year, often arising after the death of one partner (see further Bissett-Johnson and Barton 1999).

How then do attitudes to these legal issues compare in Scotland and England and Wales?

LEGAL AWARENESS AND MYTHS

To assess beliefs about common law marriage we asked:

> As far as you know do unmarried couples who live together
> for some time have a 'common law marriage' which gives
> them the same legal rights as married couples.

As in England and Wales, over half of all survey respondents in Scotland (57 per cent) thought (incorrectly) that unmarried couples did have a common law marriage which gives them the same legal rights as married couples. Whilst this does mean that over a third of the Scottish sample – 36 per cent – rightly thought there was no such legal status, it does also reveal that a sizeable portion of the population is ill-informed and may be ordering their lives around misconceived notions. On examining the views of current cohabitants, only a slightly higher percentage (58 per cent) positively believed in common law marriage in both Scotland and England and Wales. However, the number who thought there probably was no such status rose to 40 per cent in Scotland (as opposed to 37 per cent in the English and Welsh sample) with hardly any of the Scottish respondents claiming they were unsure of the position. Obviously, one reason to cohabit rather than marry may well be to avoid a Family Law-based redistribution of assets on breakdown or death and it could be that Scots are somewhat cannier on this issue! Yet, there are arguably unacceptably high levels of misperceptions in Scotland and England and Wales.

Interestingly, overall in Scotland, as in England and Wales, men were more likely to believe in the existence of common law marriage than women, with 60 per cent of men in Scotland who believed in this as opposed to 56 per cent of women. Whereas in England and Wales, the younger the respondent the more likely they are to believe that there is a legal status of common law marriage, in Scotland the youngest age group were wiser than the average respondent, with only 52 per cent believing in such a status. However, it was in the under 35 age group where the highest proportion of believers were found in Scotland (61 per cent) and also where the strongest variations were found on gender lines. For here 65 per cent of men as opposed to only 58 per cent of women thought there was such a legal status. Given this is the age group in which most cohabitation is concentrated and thus most likely to occur, such misconceptions are concerning.

However, when particular situations were put to people, proportionately fewer than those indicating belief in common law marriage were confident about its application in these contexts. The aim of the vignettes was to put scenarios where cohabitants were in a vulnerable position, legally speaking, as compared with a similar married couple. We therefore chose three areas. The first concerned the issue of financial support on relationship breakdown. In the cohabitation context, there is no possibility for a cohabitant to claim such support in this situation. However, The first scenario related to financial support on relationship breakdown, a situation where there is currently no legal right for a cohabitant to claim support. We asked:

I'd now like you to imagine an unmarried couple with no children who have been living together for ten years. Say their relationship ends. Do you think the woman should or should not have the same rights to claim for financial support from the man as she would if they had been married? And do you think she does in fact have the same rights as a married woman to claim financial support from the manor, or does she have fewer rights?

Table 4.8 Whether a cohabitant does and should have same rights as a married person in relation to financial support, property inheritance and parental consent

	Woman's right to financial support after breakdown of relationship	Right to family home after death of partner	Father's right to consent to child's medical treatment
	%	%	%
Current law			
Does have	38	35	49
Does not have	54	56	40
Don't know	8	9	12
What should happen			
Should have	68	92	98
Should not have	30	7	2
Don't know	2	1	0

sample size: 1663

As the Table 4.8 shows, a narrow majority of all respondents correctly thought that a woman in this situation would have fewer rights than a married woman, with a large minority (over a third) believing that she had the same rights. However, when we asked what the law should be, the situation more than reversed with more than two-thirds thinking that she should have the same rights to financial support, less than a third that she should not, and only a tiny group saying they did not know. The Scottish sample were even clearer in their feelings on this than their English counterparts who also endorsed the same view, but with just less than two thirds supporting it.

There would therefore seem to be clear support for long term cohabitants to be treated as married couples on relationship breakdown in Scotland.

The second scenario, involved imagining the same couple, but here they live in a house bought in the man's name. We asked:

Imagine another unmarried couple without children who have been living together for ten years and live in a house bought in the man's name. Say he dies without making a will. Do you think the woman should or should not have the same rights to remain in this home as she would if she had been married to the man? And do you think she does in fact have the same rights as a married woman to remain in this home, or, does she have fewer rights?

Again a similar proportion, 35 per cent thought incorrectly that she did such have rights, whilst 55 per cent thought she did not. However a resounding 92 per cent of Scottish respondents (exactly the same proportion as in England and Wales) thought that she should have such rights, whereas only seven per cent were against this in both jurisdictions.

Our last scenario involved the inferior status of unmarried fathers. We asked:

Now imagine another unmarried couple who have been living together for ten years. They have a child who needs medical treatment. Do you think the father should or should not have the same rights to make decisions about his child's medical treatment as he would if he was married to the child's mother? And do you think he does in fact have the same rights as a married man to make decisions about this medical treatment, or, does he have fewer rights?

Just under half (49 per cent) of our Scottish sample actually thought he did have the same rights, although as an unmarried father does not usually have parental responsibility and rights for his child, he has no authority to consent to such treatment for his child. Forty per cent were aware that he had fewer rights and a further 12 per cent did not know the position. Posed with the question of whether such an unmarried father should have the same rights, a resounding 98 per cent thought that he should, with only two per cent thinking the contrary, mirroring English and Welsh views on this issue almost exactly.

This part of the survey can be seen to have made two findings of great importance with regard to cohabitation and legal knowledge in Scotland. Firstly there are widespread misperceptions about the legal position of cohabitants with a majority of those questioned indicating that there was a general legal status of common law marriage giving them marriage-like rights. Whilst people were more aware when faced with specific scenarios that there were differences in the legal treatment of cohabitants and married couples, between a third and a half of all respondents believed that they were treated the same where cohabitation had been long-term, even though there were no children of the relationship. People were at their most confused as regards the position of unmarried cohabiting fathers, who are not treated the same as married fathers even though they may have jointly registered the child's birth. Whilst the European Court of Human Rights has ruled that this situation does not breach the European Convention on Human Rights (see McMichael v UK A/308 (1995) 20 EHHR 205) and thus the Human Rights Act 1998, there is overwhelming support for a change in the law. Indeed this is the second very significant finding of the survey. The Scottish public are even readier than their English counterparts for law reform giving cohabitants marriage-like rights and legal status.

Whether law should attempt to follow or shape social change is an issue on which there are differing shades of opinion. A further moot point is whether changes in the law can or do affect social behaviour, particularly in the realm of moral decisions. However, as Maclean and Eekelaar put it, 'Law is a purposive activity and policy makers expect results.' (Maclean and Eekelaar 1997, 7).

At Westminster, belief in the power of the law to send out messages has led them down the road of supporting marriage or family form rather than looking more broadly at those who perform the same family functions – child rearing, mutual support, financial assistance – as married families (Home Office 1998). However, whilst this decision has been taken from a standpoint where there have been large concessions already made to cohabitants in England and Wales, in Scotland the gap between the social acceptability of cohabitation as a family form and the preparedness of the law to take account of its existence at times of family crisis is far wider. Thus in England and Wales, other than in the sphere of property law, there are remedies for cohabitants of more than two years standing should their partner die without providing for them, or if there is a dispute about who should occupy the rented family home

83

on relationship breakdown. So whilst marriage is clearly privileged and the legal position is extremely confusing and complicated, cohabitants lack a formal and consistent legal status, but are not completely ignored. In Scotland on the other hand, cohabitants have been afforded few concessions, even where there are children or the relationship is one of longstanding. Their plight here has been largely ignored, with couples needing to make their own arrangements. Yet not only are people failing to do so, but the majority are unaware of the need to take matters into their own hands. Lack of Family Law provision for cohabitants has not, it seems clear, led to less ignorance of the legal position in Scotland. Given the likely increase in such relationships, these problems are set to become more and more common.

Yet should the Scottish Executive extend marriage-like rights to cohabiting couples or is this oppressive to those who are deliberately cohabiting to avoid marriage-like rights and responsibilities? If it decides to extend the focus of family law beyond the married, to whom should this extend and on what basis? What sort of balance would best fit the needs of Scottish society?

PROPOSALS AND OPTIONS FOR LEGAL REFORM

Broadly, the Scottish Executive has in its White Paper (Scottish Executive 2000, and see further Bissett-Johnson 2000) resurrected the ideas relating to cohabitation put forward by the Scottish Law Commission back in 1992 and which failed to be implemented at that point due to lack of Parliamentary time at Westminster.

COHABITING FATHERS

Whilst there is a clear political will to improve the status of at least some unmarried fathers in relation to their children, there are various ways in which this could be achieved and these were set out in the 1999 Scottish Office Consultation Paper (Scottish Office 1999). Given the acknowledged low uptake – less than two per cent (Scottish Office,1999: para. 5.4.3) – in the available but virtually unheard of parental responsibility and rights agreements, one option would be merely to conduct a publicity campaign to increase awareness about agreements and retain the status quo. At the other extreme, automatic parental responsibility and rights could be given to all fathers, whether married or unmarried. Lastly, automatic parental responsibility and rights could just be given to fathers who jointly register the birth of their child with the mother. It is in fact this last option which both the Scottish Executive and Westminster[1] propose to endorse. Whilst it was not suggested that parental responsibility and rights should be limited to unmarried cohabiting fathers, given that nearly three quarters of all joint birth registrations to unmarried parents are made by parents cohabiting at the same address (Scottish Office 1999: para 5.4.2), this is an option which would benefit cohabitants more than any other group. However, it may still mean that some cohabiting fathers who perhaps for purely practical reasons, such as work commitments, fail to attend with the mother in order to register the birth may miss out on this enhanced legal standing, and will remain ignorant of their legally inferior parental status. Given that cohabiting fathers are living with the child at birth, some thought could be given to whether this is a category which should acquire automatic status regardless of whether or not birth registration is joint.

FINANCIAL PROVISION ON DEATH OF A COHABITANT

Another proposal is to introduce a provision similar to one which does already exist in England and Wales. This is that a cohabitant should be able to claim financial provision from their deceased partner's estate where there is no will in their favour. In England and Wales, this is limited to those who have lived together for at least two years but no time qualification period is suggested in Scotland. As in England and Wales, however there would be no automatic entitlement to a share of the estate or to any payment but rather the court would have a discretion as to the amount if any that should be paid. The criteria to be applied by the court would include the length of the relationship, the existence of any children of the relationship, the size of the estate, any payment already received as a result of the death, and any economic advantage gained by the deceased at the expense of their partner or disadvantage suffered by their partner in the interests of the deceased or their children. The court would be able to pay out capital and/or transfer property and would go some way to redressing potential injustice, although not going as far as ensuring a cohabitant in this situation would be able to stay in the home, a right guaranteed to spouses. Given that there was overwhelming support for cohabitants to be treated as spouses in relation to this issue in our survey (92 per cent agreed this should be the case), perhaps the proposal whilst radical and appropriate ten years ago, does not now go far enough. A right to instigate legal action is not the same as an automatic right to continue to occupy your home. In 1992, the Scottish Law Commission gave the following reasons (Scottish Law Commission 1992: para. 16.1):

> There is, in particular, a respectable view that it would be unwise to impose marriage-like legal consequences on couples who may have deliberately chosen not to marry. It was argued by some of those who commented on the discussion paper that the best approach would be to leave those who opt out of marriage to make their own legal arrangements by means, for example, of cohabitation contracts, insurance Policies and wills. Although we have considerable sympathy with this view, we doubt whether it is realistic to expect all cohabiting couples to make adequate private legal arrangements. We accept, however, that legal intervention in this area ought to be limited and that it requires to be justified in each situation in which it is recommended. It should neither undermine marriage, nor undermine the freedom of those who have deliberately opted out of marriage.

In terms of undermining the freedom of those who have deliberately opted out of marriage, our sample of cohabitants in Scotland were strongly in favour of marriage-like rights, particularly in the context of the death of one partner. An overwhelming 91 per cent of them thought that a cohabitant of ten years standing should be able to remain in the home on the death of their partner in the same way as a spouse. Neither would such an approach be resented by the married community who among our sample were even more strongly in favour (97 per cent) of such a right. Whether awarding more rights to cohabitants would of itself undermine marriage is difficult to predict or indeed disentangle from other factors. However, the retention of a distinction has not to date prevented a sizeable increase in the incidence of cohabitation in Scotland.

OCCUPATION RIGHTS IN DOMESTIC VIOLENCE SITUATIONS

The other Scottish Executive proposal which already appertains in England and Wales is to give cohabitants improved rights and remedies similar to married couples to occupy the family home in cases of domestic violence by the extension of the 'matrimonial interdict' to those living together. In England and Wales, political compromise forced by the pro-marriage lobby resulted in a complex array of orders being adopted in Part IV Family Law Act 1996 with varying criteria according to whether the parties were married or unmarried and whether they or their partner were the legal occupants of the property. It is to be hoped that the Scottish equivalent will avoid this unnecessary complexity given the general support demonstrated for an increase in cohabitants' legal rights.

OWNERSHIP OF HOUSEHOLD GOODS AND HOUSEKEEPING MONEY

Three other proposals have been put forward by the Scottish Executive which go beyond the concessions made to cohabitants in England and Wales. Firstly, joint ownership of household goods and housekeeping money is to be extended to cohabitants in Scotland.

FINANCIAL PROVISION ON RELATIONSHIP BREAKDOWN

Secondly, although there is to be no claim for aliment on relationship breakdown, cohabitants may make a claim against their former partner where 'economic disadvantage' has been suffered by one partner in the interests of the family. Depending on how this is interpreted by the courts, such a provision would enable those (often women) who make sacrifices to their own careers and financial position in order to facilitate the well-being and earning capacity of their partner and/or the welfare of any children of the relationship. This is a radical departure and one which is not even on the agenda south of the border. It would constitute an important acknowledgment that the function of cohabiting and married families is often the same and that cohabitation can involve similar sacrifices to those recognised as occurring within marriage despite the difference in form. A notable lacuna in the Executive's proposals is that they do not proposed to introduce any mechanism whereby disputes between cohabitants on relationship breakdown relating to the rented family home can be resolved. This already exists in England and Wales and it is surprising that consideration has not been given to the need for such a remedy to be made available.

This omission may perhaps be explained in part by the inclusion in the Housing (Scotland) Act 2001 (not yet implemented) of reforms which will enable 'qualifying occupiers' (which include a cohabitant) other than the tenant to become a joint tenant of a public sector rented family home and keep the home if a tenant partner abandons it. However, neither the Act nor the proposals seemingly deal with the situation where there is a dispute as to which partner should stay in the home.

COHABITATION CONTRACTS

Private ordering of cohabitation relationships by cohabitation contract, which in both Scotland and England and Wales, are of uncertain legal effect, are to be declared valid. This again is a welcome development and will enable those cohabitants who do not wish to be regulated in the same way as married couples to make their own arrangements. Given the lack of written agreements about shares in the family home and the lack of wills made by cohabitants as revealed by the survey, however, it seems that this alone will do little to improve the position.

OTHER OPTIONS FOR REFORM

Given the strong support for cohabitants to acquire marriage-like rights, might it not be simpler to extend marriage laws to cohabitation relationships of a certain duration, whilst enabling cohabitants to contract out if they freely wished to make their own arrangements? This would amount in a way to the reinvention of common law marriage but with the safeguard of opting out. Such a system already exists in Canada (see Bailey 2001).

Another possibility is to extend marriage-like rights to those who register their cohabitation relationships and contracts. This exists in France and the Netherlands where registration is available to same- and opposite-sex couples. This effectively creates a new institution not modelled on marriage. It would avoid any undermining of marriage yet afford similar legal protection or at least prompt thought and agreement as to necessary arrangements by those in unmarried relationships with the same or similar functions to marriage.

CONCLUSION

Scotland seems to be heading for the same piecemeal solutions enacted in England and Wales, which by creating tiers of inconsistent and complex legal distinctions between married and unmarried couples, benefits no one other than the lawyers. The position in England and Wales is much criticised and proposals for reform have been put forward by both the Family Law Committee of the Law Society (1999) and by the Solicitors Family Law Association (2000), both of which propose closer assimilation of the legal status of cohabitation with marriage as opposed to a partnership registration system. What is more, piecemeal reform, while providing a safety net for cohabitants in some areas, may actually deter people from making their own arrangements and leave them in a legal wilderness in times of crisis. Given the clear support for the acceptance of and legal assimilation of cohabitation to marriage, why does Scotland not avoid this trap? The Scottish Executive proposals whilst radical when first put forward are now ten years old. Given the changed social trends away from marriage coupled with the support for extension of marriage-like rights to cohabitants, it is suggested that a better way forward would be to adopt a simpler easily understood framework of Family Law rights, where families are treated by law according to their function rather than form. Scotland already has a form of common law marriage which the Scottish Executive proposes to retain and it may be more fruitful to look at an extension of an automatic marriage-like status. But at the same time, it would be important to permit the freedom to contract out of such a framework.

It is clear from the survey that few current/past cohabitants make legal provision, and it is manifest that there is serious confusion about what the legal situation of cohabitants is. Without doubt cohabitation is viewed as an acceptable family form in Scotland which warrants the protection and remedies the law affords to the institution of marriage. Presumably this is because the public recognise that a functional approach to family regulation makes most sense in the context of the reality of today's social trends.

Whilst the proposals of the Scottish Executive do coincide with the attitudes expressed on these issues in the Scottish Social Attitudes survey, I would hazard that Scotland is in fact ready for an even more radical approach. It is to be hoped that the debate surrounding the proposals which will come when a Bill is introduced into the Scottish Parliament will range beyond the limited framework of the White Paper and provide Scotland with a functional-based pluralistic approach to family law appropriate to the 21st century which achieves fair outcomes on family matters judged on what families do within society and regardless of the form they take.

ACKNOWLEDGEMENT

The author would like to thank Professor Alastair Bissett-Johnson, Professor of Private Law, University of Dundee, for his valuable comments and assistance on the finer differences between English and Scottish Family Law.

REFERENCES

Bailey, M. (2001), 'Canadian and American Approaches to Same-sex cohabitation', paper given to Socio-Legal Studies Association annual conference April 2001, Bristol

Barlow, A. (1997), *Cohabitants and the Law*, London: Butterworth.

Bissett-Johnson, A. (2000), 'Parents and Children – A Scottish White Paper', *International Family Law*: 155, pp. 155-61.

Bissett-Johnson, A., and Barton, C. (1999), 'The similarities and differences in Scottish and English family law in dealing with changing family patterns', *Journal of Social Welfare and Family Law* 21, pp. 1-21.

Ermisch, J. and Francesconi, M. (1999), *Cohabitation in Great Britain: Not for long but Here to Stay*, Colchester: Institute for Social and Economic Research.

Haskey, J. (1999), 'Cohabitational and marital histories of adults in Great Britain', *Population Trends*, 96, pp. 13-24.

Home Office (1998), *Supporting Families: A Consultative Paper*, London: The Stationary Office.

Law Society Family Law Committee (1999), *Cohabitation – Proposals for Reform of the Law*, London: Law Society.

Maclean, M., and Eekelaar, J. (1997), *The Parental Obligation, A Study of Parenthood across Households*, Oxford: Hart Publishing.

Morgan, P. (1999), *Marriage-lite: the rise of cohabitation and its consequences*, London: Institute for the Study of Civil Society.

Scottish Executive (2000), *Parents and Children*, Edinburgh: Scottish Executive.

Scottish Law Commission (1992), *Report on Family Law*, Report no. 135, Edinburgh: HMSO.

Scottish Office (1999), *Improving Scottish Family Law*, Edinburgh: The Scottish Office.

Shaw, C. and Haskey, J. (1999), 'New estimates and projections of the population cohabiting in England and Wales', *Population Trends* 95, pp. 1-17.

Smart, C. and Stevens, P. (2000), *Cohabitation Breakdown*, London: Family Policy Studies Centre.

Solicitors Family Law Society (2000), *Fairness for Families – Proposals for Reform of the Law on Cohabitation*, Orpington: SFLA.

Wilcock, I. (2000), 'Cohabitation: An Alternative Basis', *Juridical Review* 1, pp. 1-9.

---

[1] The Adoption and Children Bill 2001 proposed to effect this change in England and Wales (see clause 91). However the Bill was lost as a result of the 2001 general election. The re-introduction of the Bill was subsequently announced in the Queen's speech but is still awaited.

5

SCOTLAND'S MORALS

ALISON PARK

INTRODUCTION

Many recent debates in Scotland have focused attention on judgements as to what is right and wrong in public and private life. The furore in 2000 over the repeal of Section 28/Clause 2a (which prohibited the 'promotion' of homosexuality in schools by local authorities) provides just one example. This led to considerable debate about Scottish attitudes towards homosexuality, about the extent to which these attitudes differ from those south of the border, and about whether or not views have hardened or softened over the years.

The then Local Government minister, Wendy Alexander, was not alone in arguing Section 28 was about far wider issues than schools and homosexuality. She saw it as being 'about the character of our society and whether Scotland is tolerant' (Alexander 2000). And the verdict of some in this regard has been scathing. Take Tim Luckhurst, a former editor of *The Scotsman*:

> The vicious campaigning and pointed personal abuse which preceded repeal has not ended in a victory for progressive thought. It has provided overwhelming proof that Scotland remains a backward, repressed and socially conservative country. (Luckhurst 2000).

Other areas have attracted, or are likely to attract, similar levels of debate – abortion, racism and euthanasia being but a few examples.

But confusion exists about quite what the public's view is on many of these issues, and how amenable these views might be to change. Thus, the Scottish Executive's experience at the hands of the 'Keep the Clause' protesters has led some to argue that the Parliament should adopt a more 'aggressive' approach on such issues in order to prevent them being hijacked by crusaders such as Brian Souter. Their view is that the public has been, or can be, won over on these matters. But others have expressed concerns about the willingness of the Scottish public to adopt such an egalitarian stance:

> What if we did present this as an issue about the new Scotland, and people turned round and said that actually they preferred the old Scotland, thanks very much. (Senior Executive member quoted in Farquharson and Robertson 2000).

Some of these debates have also been seen as illustrative of profound differences of opinion between Scotland and England. A common assumption, for instance, is that Scotland's different religious profile (particularly in relation to Catholicism) means that views north and south of the border differ radically. Broader differences between Scotland and England in relation to the church, to education and legal systems, and to the media also point towards other sources for difference in a wide range of attitudes and values (Brown, McCrone and Paterson 1998).

All these issues raise fascinating questions about attitudes and values in modern Scotland. These broadly fall into four categories. Firstly, what are Scotland's 'moral' values? What judgements do the public make about right and wrong? Answering these questions helps us avoid the all too common trap of conflating a debate's intensity (as fought in the media or parliament) with public opinion in general. Secondly, how – if at all – have attitudes and values changed over time? Are attitudes about these matters stable and unchanging – or are they constantly shifting (and, if so, in what direction)? Thirdly, are views in Scotland notably different to those held south of the border and, if so, why? Examining this issue will allow us to assess the extent to which public opinion in England and Scotland might place different pressures upon policy-makers. Finally, the chapter considers the amount of variation that exists within Scotland. Can we, for instance, even talk sensibly about Scotland's 'morals' at all, or should we be focusing far more upon the differences of view that exist within modern Scotland? With this in mind, the chapter examines the way opinion varies according to factors such as age, sex, education, and class, as well as assessing the views of those with different political and religious persuasions.

The chapter focuses on a range of issues that fall into the admittedly vague territory that is called 'morality'. It starts, perhaps not surprisingly, with religion, so long a critical arbiter of right and wrong, and assesses the role that it plays in Scotland in the 21st century, particularly when it comes to people's moral judgements. In the light of Section 28, we then consider beliefs about sexuality, focusing on attitudes towards the acceptability of premarital sex and homosexuality. Next we look at abortion, another key 'moral' issue of our times. We then consider the prevalence and variation of racial prejudice in Scotland, another subject about which much concern has been expressed. And, finally, we examine a number of measures concerned with personal honesty and the sorts of moral judgements that we all make daily in our lives.

An on-going theme throughout the chapter is the extent to which there are connections between these possibly disparate moral issues. We find that factors such as age and gender are critical for some – whereas for others they are less important. Other views vary markedly by political orientation (though not always in the direction we might expect!). To help assess the links that may exist between our different measures, we also distinguish between people with 'libertarian' and 'authoritarian' values, as measured by a series of questions about (amongst other things) tradition, order and obedience. This value dimension cuts across the more traditional left-right dimension of British political life (with there being, for example, both libertarian right-wingers and left-wingers – as well as authoritarian ones).

The chapter uses two sources of data to address these questions – the 2000 Scottish Social Attitudes survey and, for earlier years, Scottish respondents who took part in the British Social Attitudes survey series.

RELIGION

Andrew O'Hagan once remarked that 'religion is everything in Scotland' (O'Hagan 2000). It has certainly played a central role in many of the recent debates about issues such as abortion and homosexuality, as well as provoking considerable discussion in its own right (as illustrated by the controversy ignited by James

MacMillan's accusation about Scotland's 'sleep-walking bigotry' in relation to Catholics). So we begin by examining religious attachment and practice in Scotland; in particular, the extent to which people regard themselves as belonging to a religion and how, if at all, this has changed over time. We shall turn later on in the chapter to how views about a range of issues vary according to one's religious affiliation.

As Table 5.1 shows, a majority – nearly six in ten people – see themselves as belonging to a religion, and four in ten do not. Around one third belong to the Church of Scotland, one in nine to the Catholic church, and one in ten to another Christian religion.[1]

Table 5.1 Religious attachment 1983 and 2000

	1983	2000
	%	%
No religion	29	41
Church of Scotland	40	35
Catholic	22	12
Other Christian	9	10
Other religion	0	1
Sample size	184	1663

One of the most striking features of the table is the vivid picture it paints of change over time. The ranks of those who do not see themselves as belonging to a religion at all have swelled dramatically (up 12 points from 29 per cent), and the proportion of those who are religiously inclined has fallen. This has had a disproportionate effect on Catholicism, with the proportion of Catholics in Scotland nearly halving between 1983 and 2000.

Of course, religious attachment tells us little about the importance of religion in people's lives. Perhaps, for instance, declining religious attachment simply reflects the falling away of the less committed – who, in the past, would describe themselves as religious but might – for instance – rarely attend services. But, as Table 5.2 shows, this picture is far from true. While in 1983 one third of the religious attended services connected with their religion every week, now less than one quarter do so. Meanwhile the proportion who go to services less often than once a year has doubled to two in every five. So any overall decline in church attendance in Scotland as a whole is not only due to an increasing proportion of people turning away from religion itself – it also reflects the fact that the religious are going less often than they did in the past.

Table 5.2 Religious attendance 1983 and 2000

	1983	2000
	%	%
Once a week or more	33	23
At least once a month	18	13
At least once a year	25	21
Less often than once a year or never	21	42
Sample size	129	1003

Table 5.3 Religious attachment, Scotland and England 2000

	Scotland	England
	%	%
No religion	41	40
Church of Scotland	35	1
Church of England	3	33
Catholic	12	9
Other Christian	7	12
Other religion	1	5
Sample size	1663	2887

A common assumption is that religion plays a more important role in Scotland than in England. But, whether this is true or not, religious attachment north and south of the border is notable far more for its similarity than for its difference (Table 5.3) In both countries around four in ten say they do not belong to a religion and around one third subscribe to the Church of England or the Church of Scotland. Only in relation to Catholicism and non-Christian religions do the two countries differ (with Scotland having a higher proportion of Catholics and a lower proportion of those belonging to non-Christian religions).

Despite the similarity in their religious profile, Scotland and England do differ when it comes to religious attendance, with Scots being the more frequent attenders (Table 5.4). But this difference is now far less marked than it has been in the past. In 1983, for instance, nearly twice as many in Scotland (33 per cent) than in England (17 per cent) attended services at least once a week or more. By 2000 this gap had shrunk to six percentage points. Meanwhile, the proportion who never attend services, while still slightly higher in England than Scotland, increased in Scotland by 19 percentage points over this period, compared with a six point increase in England.

One possible explanation for this difference between Scotland and England in church attendance relates to the different religious profiles of the two countries (Brown 1997). As we have seen, Scotland has a higher proportion of Catholics, and Catholics are more likely than many other religious groups to attend services frequently. This explanation is not, however, sufficient to explain the differences we have found. While it is certainly true that Catholics are the most likely to attend services weekly (47 per cent of Catholics do so, compared with 15 per cent of those belonging to the Church of Scotland), the religious profiles of Scotland and England are not sufficiently different for this to explain the different levels of attendance we have found. Even when we restrict attention to particular groups, attendance is higher in Scotland. There, for instance, 47 per cent of Catholics attend services at least once a week, compared with only 30 per cent of Catholics in England.

**Table 5.4 Religious attendance, Scotland and England,
1983 and 2000**

	Scotland		England	
	1983	2000	1983	2000
	%	%	%	%
Once a week or more	33	23	17	17
Never	17	36	38	42
Sample size	129	1003	992	1752

There are considerable variations throughout Scotland in religiosity – both in terms of people's religious attachment and their attendance. The biggest differences of all are age-related (Table 5.5). Older groups are much more likely than younger ones to belong to a religion (and, if they do, to attend services frequently). It is these stark differences between the generations that largely explain the gradual decline in religious attachment and attendance over the decades, as older – more religious – generations die out and are replaced by younger – less religious – ones (Park 2000).

Table 5.5 Religion and age 2000

	% who do not belong to a religion	Sample size	% belonging to religion who attend weekly services	Sample size
18-24	63	144	13	54
25-34	61	295	13	114
35-44	48	333	27	171
45-54	34	257	19	165
55-64	25	229	23	171
65+	20	404	31	327

There are also considerable gender differences in religiosity. Women are both more likely than men to belong to a religion and, when they do, to attend frequently. One half of men do not belong to a religion, but only one third of women (34 per cent).

Class and educational differences also exist, but are less pronounced than those linked to either age or gender (Table 5.6). Intriguingly, they cut across one another, so that those with degrees are more likely to be not religious than those without qualifications, as are those in manual occupations when compared to non-manual ones.

Table 5.6 Religion and education and class 2000

	% who do not belong to a religion	Sample size	% belonging to religion who attend weekly services	Sample size
Degree	45	214	35	114
No qualifications	33	556	23	380
Non-manual	40	792	26	482
Manual	45	705	20	401

Religious attachment and attendance also varies according to a person's party political identification (Table 5.7). Conservative identifiers are the most likely to describe themselves as belonging to a religion and Scottish National Party and Liberal Democrat identifiers the least. That said, although Liberal Democrats are less likely than average to belong to a religion, those who do are more likely than other groups to attend on a weekly basis. Multivariate analysis techniques (which take account of the inter-relationships between different characteristics) suggest that this reflects the educational profile of Liberal Democrat supporters; those with higher educational qualifications are more likely than average to attend services frequently – and a disproportionate number of this group are also Liberal Democrat supporters.

Table 5.7 Religion and party identification 2000

	% who do not belong to a religion	Sample size	% belonging to religion who attend weekly services	Sample size
Conservative	27	269	22	206
Labour	39	621	25	386
Liberal Democrat	46	121	28	71
Scottish National Party	49	319	13	158

Members of different religious groups also vary in their scores on our libertarian-authoritarian scale, with the religious being more authoritarian in their outlook than those who are not religious at all.

So far, then, we have seen that a majority of Scots continue to see themselves as belonging to a religion – but this proportion is falling fast, as are levels of church attendance amongst them. There are considerable variations within Scotland, with some groups (particularly older ones) showing high levels of religious attachment, but amongst others this is far less common. And the oft-cited differences between Scotland and England, though present, are not perhaps of the magnitude that is often imagined.

We return to religion at regular intervals throughout this chapter, focusing particularly on the extent to which moral views and judgements vary from one religious group to another. But now we turn to the issue that single-handedly attracts the most vociferous debate about morals – that of sexual behaviour.

SEXUALITY

The furore early in 2000 surrounding the repeal of Section 28 led to considerable debate about Scottish attitudes towards homosexuality. Two particular questions emerged from this debate. Firstly, to what extent – if at all – can the intensity of debate in Scotland be seen as reflective of attitudes which fundamentally differ to those held south of the border? And, secondly, to what extent might views on these

100

matters have changed over time? Has, as some have claimed, devolution 'encouraged a reawakening of premodern ideas about deviancy, law and sexual conduct' (Luckhurst 2001)?

We can assess this by examining responses to a number of questions about different types of sexual relationships (described in the Table 5.8). This shows that attitudes towards homosexuality are more polarised than those towards other sexual relationships. Thus, while clear majorities condemn sexual relationships involving people under 16 or extra-marital relationships, and clear majorities see pre-marital sex as perfectly acceptable, opinion on homosexuality is more divided. Around four in ten describe it as being always wrong, while the same proportion take the view that it is rarely or never wrong.

Table 5.8 Attitudes towards different types of sexual relationship 2000

	boy and girl under 16	extra-marital	adults of same sex	before marriage
	%	%	%	%
Always wrong	68	65	39	8
Mostly or sometimes wrong	28	31	17	17
Rarely or not at all wrong	3	2	38	71
Sample size	1663	1663	1663	1663

Although views about homosexuality remain divided, they have become substantially more liberal over the last two decades, with the proportion thinking homosexuality is always wrong falling by 19 points in nearly as many years. This liberal shift is also evident when considering attitudes to pre-marital sex, with the proportion taking the least accepting view of this more than halving between 1983 and 2000.

As shown below, there is certainly little evidence to suggest that attitudes towards homosexuality are hardening over time. What then of the claim that attitudes in Scotland are less liberal than those in England? This certainly seems to have been the case in the past (Table 5.9) – in 1983, for instance, 58 per cent thought that homosexuality was always wrong, compared with 48 per cent in England. But now views in the two countries are broadly similar. So there is little sign so far of any backlash, whether prompted by devolution or not.

Table 5.9 Attitudes to homosexuality and premarital sex, Scotland and England 1983 and 2000

	Scotland		England	
	1983	2000	1983	2000
% 'always wrong'				
Homosexual sex	58	39	48	36
Premarital sex	21	8	16	8
Sample size	183	1663	1449	2887

Table 5.10 Attitudes towards homosexuality and premarital sex, by age 2000

	% homosexuality 'always wrong'	% premarital sex 'always wrong'	Sample size
18-24	18	1	144
25-34	24	1	295
35-44	30	3	333
45-54	39	5	257
55-64	53	12	229
65+	66	26	404

Enormous variations exist throughout Scottish society in attitudes towards homosexuality and premarital sex. Nowhere is the gulf wider than between young and old (Table 5.10). The young have the most permissive stance, with fewer than one in five thinking that homosexuality is always wrong (compared with two thirds of the 65 or older age group). But, perhaps not surprisingly, the discrepancy between these age groups is at its greatest in relation to sex before marriage – seen as always wrong by one in four aged 65 or more but only one in a hundred of 18-24 year olds (a total of two respondents in this age group!). As is the case with religion, these age differences are a clear factor driving increasing social liberalism when it comes to sexual matters – with younger, more tolerant, generations gradually replacing their less tolerant predecessors.

Although men and women do not differ significantly in their views about premarital sex, men take a much more critical stance of homosexuality than women, with nearly half (48 per cent) seeing it as always wrong, compared with only one third of women (32 per cent). This difference occurs in all age groups, meaning that the most liberal views of all are held by young women (only 12 per cent of whom take the most critical view of homosexuality, compared with 27 per cent of young men) and the least liberal views held by men aged 65 or more (three quarters of whom think homosexuality is always wrong).

One of the groups most frequently alluded to in the debates surrounding the abolition or retention of Section 28 were parents, and it does appear that parents generally have more critical views of homosexuality than non-parents, even when age differences between these groups are taken into account. For instance, if we focus only on those aged between 35 and 44, nearly one third of parents (32 per cent) take the view that homosexuality is always wrong, compared with 22 per cent of non-parents. Still, amongst parents a higher proportion – 44 per cent – think homosexuality is rarely wrong or not wrong at all, so it would be wrong to imagine that parents are any more united on this issue than any other group.

Attitudes also vary according to a person's educational and occupational characteristics, particularly in relation to attitudes to homosexuality (Table 5.11). Those with degree level qualifications or working in non-manual occupations have the most liberal views, and those with no qualifications at all or in manual jobs have the least. The religious are more likely than the non-religious to have a critical view of homosexuality. Note, however, that Catholics are slightly more accepting both of homosexuality and pre-marital sex than are people belonging to other religious groups.

Table 5.11 Attitudes towards homosexuality and premarital sex, by education, socio-economic group and religion 2000

	% homosexuality 'always wrong'	% premarital sex 'always wrong'	Sample size
Degree	19	7	214
No qualifications	56	12	556
Non-manual socio-economic group	33	7	792
Manual socio-economic group	47	9	705
Church of Scotland	44	12	599
Catholic	41	5	206
Other Christian	48	20	178
No religion	31	2	660

In terms of party preferences (Table 5.12), Conservative identifiers are by far the most illiberal – in relation both to homosexuality and to premarital sex. On homosexuality the views of Labour and Nationalist identifiers are broadly similar, with Liberal Democrats having the most liberal views of all.

Not surprisingly, there is a strong relationship between a person's views about sexuality and their position on the libertarian-authoritarian scale; those who are critical of homosexuality and premarital sex have more authoritarian views generally than those who are not critical (Table 5.13).

Table 5.12 Attitudes towards homosexuality and premarital sex, by party identification 2000

	% homosexuality 'always wrong'	% premarital sex 'always wrong'	Sample size
Conservative	52	12	269
Labour	38	7	621
Liberal Democrat	30	8	121
SNP	37	5	319

Table 5.13 Attitudes towards homosexuality and premarital sex, by score on the libertarian-authoritarian scale 2000

	Mean score libertarian-authoritarian scale	Sample size	Standard error
Homosexuality 'always wrong'	4.02	600	.039
Homosexuality 'not wrong at all'	3.46	452	.040
Premarital sex 'always wrong'	4.16	133	.073
Premarital sex 'not wrong at all'	3.67	879	.030

Note: a higher score on the libertarian-authoritarian scale indicates a more authoritarian outlook, a lower one a more libertarian view.

In summary then, our findings in relation to homosexuality and premarital sex have much in common with those on religion – evidence of rapid change over time (in this case in a liberal direction), marked variation amongst different groups in Scottish society, and very little difference between Scotland and England in contrast to the differences that were apparent in the past.

105

ABORTION

The omission of abortion from the list of devolved powers granted to Holyrood under the Scotland Act 1998 remains contentious, with many seeing it as inconsistent to devolve health and the legal system while restricting decisions about abortion to Westminster. But concerns remain that differences in mass and elite opinion between England and Scotland could result in divergent legislation.

Views about abortion will often vary according to the circumstances involved. In order to assess people's views we asked whether they thought it was wrong or not for a woman to have an abortion in two particular circumstances: firstly, if there was 'a strong chance of a serious defect in the baby'; and, secondly, if the family had 'a very low income and could not afford any more children'. As Table 5.14 shows, there is a greater tolerance of abortion on medical than social grounds but, even in the case of our 'social' scenario, only four in ten take the most restrictive view – that abortion is almost always wrong. This does not suggest that the late Cardinal Winning's scheme to encourage women in financial hardship not to have abortions is backed by any deep-rooted public abhorrence of abortion on non-medical grounds.

Table 5.14 Attitudes to abortion 2000

	If chance of a serious defect	If can't afford more children
	%	%
Almost always wrong or always wrong	16	38
Sometimes wrong	21	18
Not wrong at all	52	28
Sample size	1506	1506

Comparing views in Scotland to those in England shows no essential difference in opinion about the acceptability of abortion. This is demonstrated in Table 5.15 in relation to the permissibility of abortion on income grounds (though similar findings exist in relation to abortion on medical grounds). There is certainly little to imply that distinctive attitudes amongst the Scottish public as a whole might, were abortion a devolved power, force the Parliament to introduce new legislation.

Table 5.15 Attitudes to abortion on grounds of low income, Scotland and England 2000

	Scotland	England
	%	%
Almost always wrong or always wrong	38	37
Sometimes wrong	18	20
Not wrong at all	28	31
Sample size	1506	2515

Unfortunately, we do not have enough measures of attitudes to abortion in Scotland over time to be able to assess the extent to which they have changed. However, data for Britain as a whole shows clearly that attitudes have become notably more permissive over the last two decades and, furthermore, that this change has affected all groups within society. This is likely to reflect the fact that abortion has become more widespread and, perhaps, more of a feminist issue (Park 1999; Scott 1990).

Attitudes to abortion are not as clearly linked to age as some of the other issues discussed in this chapter. Nor do the views of men and women vary markedly. There are some class differences, with non-manual groups being more supportive than manual ones, but the most dramatic variation relates to education (Table 5.16). The two key groups in this respect are those with degrees, who adopt the most liberal stance, and those without any qualifications, who adopt the least liberal one. Thus, while nearly four in ten graduates (39 per cent) consider abortion on social grounds not to be wrong at all, fewer than one quarter (23 per cent) of those without qualifications agree.

The clearest differences in view relate to religion, with Catholics being by far the least likely to see either medical or social abortion as acceptable. Only one in four, for example, take the view that abortion is not at all wrong if there is a strong chance of a defect in the baby, compared with around one in two (or more) amongst all other groups. Despite these very specific views, Catholics do not form a sufficiently large group within the Scottish population to have a marked impact on attitudes as a whole (hence the remarkable similarity of views north and south of the border). Moreover, such beliefs are only found amongst current Catholics; they are not shared by those who were brought up Catholic but who no longer consider themselves to be so.

Table 5.16 Attitudes towards abortion, by education, class and religion 2000

% 'not wrong at all'	Abortion where chance of serious defect	Abortion where can't afford more children	Sample size
Degree	60	39	202
No qualifications	45	23	488
Non-manual socio-economic group	56	31	723
Manual socio-economic group	49	26	638
Church of Scotland	55	27	544
Catholic	22	9	178
Other Christian	46	26	163
No religion	60	35	607

Views about the acceptability of abortion also vary by party identification, but not quite in the way we might expect from our previous findings. Earlier we saw that Conservative identifiers are the most likely to be religious and are the most condemning of both homosexuality and premarital sex. By contrast, on the subject of abortion Conservative identifiers are at the more liberal end of the spectrum (as are Liberal Democrats), with Labour and SNP supporters being the most critical. Although the disapproval of

Labour supporters is, to a large extent, a reflection of the disproportionate number of Catholics amongst this group, the views of SNP supporters can not be explained in these terms.

Table 5.17 Attitudes towards abortion, by party 2000

% 'not wrong at all'	Abortion where chance of serious defect	Abortion where can't afford more children	Sample size
Conservative	60	35	253
Labour	50	26	552
Liberal Democrat	63	35	107
SNP	52	26	297

Table 5.18 Attitudes towards abortion, by score on the libertarian-authoritarian scale 2000

	Mean score libertarian-authoritarian scale	Sample size	Standard error
Abortion if chance of serious defect 'always wrong'	4.02	151	0.86
Abortion if chance of serious defect 'not wrong at all'	3.69	769	.027
Abortion if can't afford more children 'always wrong'	3.85	349	.044
Abortion if can't afford more children 'not wrong at all'	3.65	423	.038

Note: a higher score on the libertarian-authoritarian scale indicates a more authoritarian outlook, a lower one a more libertarian view.

Generally speaking, those who are most critical of abortion have more authoritarian attitudes generally than those who are more tolerant (Table 5.18). This is particularly evident when considering those who are critical of abortion on medical grounds.

Just as was the case with attitudes to homosexuality and premarital sex, these findings show very little difference between Scotland and England, and considerable variation within Scotland as a whole (although, unusually, age is not a key factor in this). And, as was the case with attitudes to sexuality, those who are most disapproving generally have a more authoritarian outlook than those who are more tolerant.

RACIAL PREJUDICE

Attitudes to homosexuality can be seen as part of a more general set of values to do with acceptance of difference and tolerance of others. Racial prejudice provides another example, and is an area of increasing concern to many, including Deputy First Minister Jim Wallace who, in responding to the results of the Stephen Lawrence Inquiry, argued that:

> for far too long we have been complacent in Scotland, seeing racism as an English problem. We have prided ourselves on our tolerance while ignoring the fear and suffering within our own ethnic minority communities, whether caused by overt racial harassment or by the unwitting insensitivity, ignorance and thoughtlessness of institutionalised racism. (Scottish Executive 1999).

Since then, of course, concern has been expressed about the prevalence of racism within certain areas of Scotland (de Lima 2001; Kelly 2000) and, as in England, about the treatment of newly arrived asylum seekers.[2]

Measuring prejudice through a survey is difficult, but has been done before (Airey 1984). To capitalise on this earlier work, we repeated a long-standing series of questions which begin by asking respondents a number of general questions about racism in Scotland, and then asking 'How would you describe yourself? As very prejudiced against people of other races, a little prejudiced, or not prejudiced at all?' By this measure, nearly one in five people describe themselves as prejudiced in some way, a small decline on the measure we obtained when we first asked this question in 1983 (Table 5.19).

Table 5.19 Self-rated racial prejudice 1983 and 2000

	1983	2000
	%	%
Very prejudiced	1	1
A little prejudiced	21	17
Not prejudiced at all	78	82
Sample size	182	1663

Table 5.20 Equal opportunities for ethnic minority groups 2000

	All	Prejudiced	Not prejudiced
Equal opportunities for ethnic minorities:	%	%	%
Gone too far	31	50	26
About right	37	31	38
Not gone far enough	27	14	29
Sample size	1663	292	1360

Opinion is divided on the issue of equal opportunities for ethnic minority groups (Table 5.20). We asked people whether they thought 'attempts to give equal opportunities to black people and Asians in Britain have gone too far or not gone far enough'. Nearly one third think that such attempts have gone too far and a similar proportion that they have not gone far enough. The most common view, held by 37 per cent, is that current attempts are about right. Not surprisingly, responses vary according to respondents' self-rated racial prejudice: those who say that they are racially prejudiced are twice as likely to think that equal opportunities for ethnic minorities have gone too far as those who say they are not racially prejudiced.

Although a significant minority do describe themselves as having a degree of prejudice, there does appear to be some truth in the notion that Scotland has lower levels of racial prejudice than England, where over one quarter of people describe themselves as being prejudiced (Table 5.21). Scots are also less likely than those in England to think that equal opportunities for ethnic minority groups have gone too far. However, any 'gap' between England and Scotland in prejudice is narrowing – between 1983 and 2000 self-rated prejudice in England fell more sharply than it did in Scotland, bringing the two countries closer together in their views.

Table 5.21 Self-rated racial prejudice, Scotland and England 1983 and 2000

| | Scotland | | England | |
	1983	2000	1983	2000
Very prejudiced	1	1	5	2
A little prejudiced	21	17	33	25
Not prejudiced at all	76	82	61	72
Sample size	182	1663	1449	1928

This fall in self-rated prejudice is not reflected in public perceptions. As Table 5.22 shows, a higher proportion of people in Scotland than in England think that racial prejudice has increased over the past five years. However, the fact that prejudice in England has fallen more rapidly than in Scotland (albeit from a higher starting point) does appear to have affected perceptions in England over time – with the proportion there who think that prejudice has increased falling from 46 to 32 per cent between 1983 and 2000.

Table 5.22 Perceptions of racial prejudice, Scotland and England 1983 and 2000

| | Scotland | | England | |
	1983	2000	1983	2000
More prejudice now than five years ago	40	39	46	32
Less prejudice now	16	17	16	24
About the same level of prejudice	41	39	36	41
Sample size	182	1663	1449	1928

Unlike many of the issues discussed in this chapter, racial prejudice varies very little from one group to another (Table 5.23). Age, so commonly linked to substantial attitudinal differences, is barely linked to prejudice at all. The same applies to education. And, although non-manual groups have slightly lower levels of prejudice (16 per cent) than manual ones (20 per cent), this difference is not particularly marked. More notable, however, is that men are more likely to admit to prejudice than women (22 and 15 per cent respectively).

Attitudes towards equal opportunities for ethnic minorities vary more than self-expressed prejudice. Older groups are more likely than younger ones to think that attempts to promote equal opportunities have gone too far, as are manual workers and, most notably, those without degree-level qualifications.

More pronounced differences emerge when we look at religion. Neither Catholics nor members of the Church of Scotland differ significantly in their views from those who are not religious. But, the small group of Christians who do not describe themselves as belonging to the Church of Scotland or the Catholic church are more likely to say that they are racially prejudiced, 28 per cent doing so (compared with 19 per cent of the Church of Scotland, 14 per cent of Catholics and 16 per cent of those with no religious affiliations).[3]

113

Table 5.23 Self-rated racial prejudice and attitudes to equal opportunities, by age, class and education 2000

	% not racially prejudiced	% think equal opportunities have 'gone too far'	Sample size
18-24	83	24	144
25-34	82	24	295
35-44	84	30	333
45-54	80	35	257
55-64	80	35	229
65+	80	35	404
Non-manual	84	29	792
Manual	80	33	705
Degree	85	17	214
No qualifications	83	34	556

Although self-rated prejudice does not seem to vary markedly by socio-economic or demographic characteristics, the same cannot be said when we look at those with different political persuasions (Table 5.24). In particular, Conservative and Nationalist identifiers are more likely to say they are racially prejudiced than are Labour or Liberal Democrats. They are also more likely to think that attempts to improve the position of ethnic minorities through equal opportunities legislation has gone too far. However, there is no relationship between racial prejudice and national identity – prejudice does not vary according to whether a person sees themselves as being Scottish rather than British (and vice versa).

Perhaps surprisingly, the racially prejudiced are not significantly any more authoritarian on our scale than those who are not prejudiced, though it is likely that this partly reflects the sample sizes involved (Table 5.25). However, those who think equal opportunities have gone too far have a more authoritarian outlook than those who think that they have not gone far enough.

Table 5.24 Self-rated racial prejudice and attitudes to equal opportunities, by party identification 2000

	% racially prejudiced	% think equal opportunities have 'gone too far'	Sample size
Conservative	26	35	269
Labour	14	25	621
Liberal Democrat	15	27	121
SNP	22	37	319

Table 5.25 Self-rated racial prejudice and attitudes to equal opportunities, by score on the libertarian-authoritarian scale 2000

	Mean score libertarian-authoritarian scale	Sample size	Standard error
Racially prejudiced	3.85	272	.054
Not racially prejudiced	3.74	1227	.026
Thinks equal opportunities for ethnic minorities has gone too far	3.96	454	.041
Thinks equal opportunities for ethnic minorities has not gone far enough	3.56	408	.045

Note: a higher score on the libertarian-authoritarian scale indicates a more authoritarian outlook, a lower one a more libertarian view.

The key findings of this, albeit cursory, look at racial prejudice in Scotland suggest that prejudice is indeed slightly lower in Scotland than in England, and that levels fell slightly between 1983 and 2000. We also found a remarkable lack of variation throughout Scottish society, although some notable differences exist in relation to party identification and – to a lesser extent – a person's general authoritarian-libertarian stance. It will clearly be important to return to this subject in the future, preferably with a wider range of questions than are currently available at our disposal, in order to explore these issues in more detail.

PERSONAL MORALITY

So far this chapter has focused on examples of the judgements of right and wrong that people make about particular types of behaviour, and on tolerance, as evidenced by attitudes towards ethnic minorities. But one of the most common ways in which the notion of 'morality' is evoked relates to honesty in people's dealings with one another, the assumption usually being that standards have declined over time. To assess this we asked respondents to give their views about a number of different situations:

> A householder is having a repair job done by a local plumber. He is told that if he pays cash, he will not be charged VAT. So he pays cash.

> A man gives a £5 note for goods he is buying in a corner shop. By mistake, he is given change for a £10 note. He notices, but keeps the change.

> A person in paid work takes on an extra weekend job and is paid in cash. He does not declare it for tax and so is £100 in pocket.

In each case we also asked what the respondent would do in the same situation.

As Table 5.26 shows, there is a clear sliding scale on these matters – with people appearing to be more judgmental about situations involving a clear victim (Johnston 1988). Thus, while around one half of the respondents see little wrong with paying cash to avoid VAT or not declaring earnings in order to avoid tax, only one in ten takes this view about keeping the wrong change in a corner shop. Reassuringly, people's expected behaviour demonstrates a similar pattern with a clear majority saying that they might pay cash to avoid VAT and only one in six that they would keep the wrong change.

Table 5.26 Judgements of wrongdoing 2000

	Pay cash so no VAT	Not declare earnings	Keep wrong change
	%	%	%
Nothing wrong/a bit wrong	55	46	10
Wrong	33	39	47
Seriously/very seriously wrong	11	15	40
Proportion who might do this themselves	63	47	14
Sample size	1663	1663	1663

Table 5.27 Avoiding VAT by paying cash 1987 and 2000

	1987	2000
	%	%
Nothing wrong/a bit wrong	51	55
Wrong	41	33
Seriously/very seriously wrong	7	11
Proportion who might do this themselves	67	63
Sample size	144	1663

How have these judgements about right and wrong changed over time? When it comes to judgements about VAT avoidance, there has been remarkably little change since 1987, when the question was first asked (Table 5.27).[4] Is there any evidence that Scotland is more or less honest than England? On two of our three scenarios (VAT avoidance and keeping the wrong change) Scots adopted a slightly more critical view than did those in England (though in all cases the differences were only in the region of four or five percentage points), and were also less likely to say they would behave in the same way themselves (Table 5.28).

Table 5.28 Keeping the wrong change in a corner shop, Scotland and England 1987 and 2000

	Scotland		England	
	1987	2000	1987	2000
	%	%	%	%
Nothing wrong or a bit wrong	11	10	17	16
Wrong	67	47	64	48
Seriously or very seriously wrong	21	40	19	36
Might you do this yourself?	10	14	11	17
Sample size	144	1663	1171	1928

Table 5.29 Keeping the wrong change in a corner shop, by age and gender 2000

	% 'seriously wrong' to keep wrong change	% who would keep change themselves	Sample size
18-24	16	26	144
25-34	26	25	295
35-44	34	16	333
45-54	43	8	257
55-64	51	7	229
65+	62	3	404
Men	36	16	691
Women	43	12	972

Critical judgements about these matters vary considerably from one group to another. This applies to all the scenarios considered but for brevity's sake we illustrate them only in relation to the

118

scenario concerned with keeping the wrong change (Table 5.29). In particular, older people are substantially more likely to be critical than the young, and are also less likely to say that they would themselves keep the change in the same situation. Thus, one quarter of 18-24 year olds would keep the wrong change, three times as many as amongst the 45 and over age group. And women are both more critical, and less likely to do this themselves, than men.

Views also vary according to religious background, but not perhaps as much as we might expect (Table 5.30). In the case of keeping the wrong change, the most critical are those who belong to the Church of Scotland, and the least critical are those who have no religion at all (though it is likely that this partly reflects this group's younger than average age profile). There were no notable differences by party identification.

Table 5.30 Judgements of wrongdoing, by religion 2000

	% 'seriously wrong' to keep wrong change	% who would keep change themselves	Sample size
Church of Scotland	48	8	599
Catholic Church	37	17	206
Other Christian	41	10	178
No religion	34	19	660

Judgements also varied according to a person's position on the libertarian-authoritarian scale, with the most critical also tending to be more authoritarian in their general outlook (Table 5.31). Similarly, those who said that they would themselves do this are less authoritarian than those who would not.

119

Table 5.31 Judgements of wrongdoing, by score on the libertarian-authoritarian scale 2000

	Mean score libertarian-authoritarian scale	Sample size	Standard error
Nothing wrong/ a bit wrong to keep wrong change in shop	3.65	199	.067
Seriously wrong to keep wrong change in shop	3.88	622	.031
Respondent would keep wrong change in shop	3.65	203	.068
Respondent would not keep wrong change in shop	3.78	1286	.026

Note: a higher score on the libertarian-authoritarian scale indicates a more authoritarian outlook, a lower one a more libertarian view.

SCOTLAND'S MORAL CODE?

Some of these findings will be surprising to those who have erroneously taken the intensity of debate surrounding issues such as homosexuality and abortion to be indicative of public opinion in Scotland more generally.

A number of general themes emerge. Firstly, views and behaviour on such matters are varied, and do not always confirm to quite what we might expect. On abortion and homosexuality, for instance, substantial proportions in Scotland are very accepting and tolerant (though it is equally true that others are less so). Moreover, considerable variation exists, making it highly dangerous to assume that the views of one particular group are common to all. In general, the young, those with degree level qualifications, non-manual workers, and those who are not religious tend to be more tolerant than average of abortion and homosexuality – and more likely to adopt fairly 'relaxed' views about personal 'honesty'. It is also clear that those with more authoritarian attitudes in general are more likely to have critical views about homosexuality, abortion, and equal opportunities for ethnic minorities. This group also has the strictest views about personal 'honesty' and probity.

Secondly, views are changing quickly – often as a result of generational change. Over the last two decades, for example, Scottish society has become more tolerant of homosexuality, less religious, and slightly less racially prejudiced. In relation to attitudes to homosexuality and religious behaviour, there is a strong chance that attitudes will continue to shift in the future.

Thirdly, there is barely any evidence of a gulf between views north and south of the border. On issues such as abortion and homosexuality no notable differences exist at all, and, even when it comes to religion, the differences are small ones (and appear to be getting smaller over time). Certainly, concern that differences in public opinion might lead to divergent policy in these areas appears unfounded.

REFERENCES

Airey, C. (1984), 'Social and moral values', in R. Jowell and C. Airey (eds), *British Social Attitudes: the 1984 Report*, Aldershot: Gower, pp. 121-56.

Alexander, W. (2000), quoted on BBC News Online (www.news.bbc.co./hi/english/uk/scotland/newsid_769000/76410.stm)

Brown, A., McCrone, D. and Paterson, L. (1998), *Politics and Society in Scotland*, Basingstoke: Macmillan.

Brown, C. G. (1997), *Religion and Society in Scotland since 1707*, Edinburgh: Edinburgh University Press.

de Lima, P. (2001), *Rural Racism in Scotland: Needs not numbers*, London: Commission for Racial Equality.

Farquharson, K. and Robertson, J. (2000), 'Morality play', *The Sunday Times*, 19th March 2000.

Johnston, M. (1988), 'The price of honesty', in R. Jowell, S. Witherspoon and L. Brook (eds), *British Social Attitudes: the 5th Report*, Aldershot: Gower, pp. 1-16.

Kelly, E. (2000), 'Racism, police and courts and Scotland', *Scottish Affairs*, Winter 2000, no. 30, pp. 141-159.

Luckhurst, T. (2001), 'Scotland returns to the Dark Ages', *New Statesman*, 21st May 2001.

Luckhurst, T. (2000), 'Backward, repressed and conservative', *The Independent*, 22nd June 2000.

O'Hagan, A. (2000), 'Into the ferment', in T. Devine (ed.), *Scotland's Shame? Bigotry and sectarianism in modern Scotland*, Edinburgh: Mainstream Publishing, pp. 25-28.

Park, A. (2000), 'The generation game', in R. Jowell, J. Curtice, A. Park, K. Thomson, L. Jarvis, C. Bromley and N. Stratford (eds), *British Social Attitudes: the 17th Report*, London: Sage, pp. 1-22.

Park, A. (1999), 'Young people and political apathy', in R, Jowell, J. Curtice, A. Park and K. Thomson (eds), *British Social Attitudes: the 16th Report*, Aldershot: Ashgate, pp. 23-44.

Scott, J. (1990), 'Women and the family', in R. Jowell, S. Witherspoon, L. Brook and B. Taylor (eds), *British Social Attitudes: the 7th Report*, Aldershot: Dartmouth, pp. 51-76.

Scottish Executive (1999), 'Wallace declares war on Scottish racism', Scottish Executive News Release, 20th July 1999.

---

[1] The 10 per cent of respondents classified as belonging to another Christian religion fall, as would be expected, into a range of different groups. Roughly one third belong to the Anglican church, a similar proportion simply call themselves 'Christian' without specifying a denomination, and the remainder are divided between a range of groups (Baptists, Methodists etc).

[2] Note that the fieldwork for the latest survey (summer 2000) was carried out before the publicity surrounding the treatment of asylum seekers in Sighthill, Glasgow.

[3] Because of the small numbers of respondents within the 'other Christian' category (172) it is difficult to investigate this difference further. That said, two groups within this category appear to be driving this finding – those who belong to the Church of England and to 'other Protestant' churches.

[4] On the subject of keeping the wrong change in a corner shop, there has been a substantial shift in a more 'honest' direction between 1987 and 2000. However, it is likely that at least part of this change reflects the different contexts within which the questions were asked in the two years; for this reason the differences are not commented upon further.

6

SOCIETY AND DEMOCRACY: THE NEW SCOTLAND

PAULA SURRIDGE

INTRODUCTION

Earlier chapters have considered a number of different areas of social life in Scotland. This chapter considers the more directly political elements of Scottish public life, in particular changes in attitudes towards the Scottish Parliament. At the time of the referendum on the setting up of the Scottish Parliament the Scottish people and politicians had high expectations of what the Parliament would deliver in Scotland (Brown et al 1999) These expectations were high regarding what the Parliament would do both in terms of policies and also in terms of how the establishment of the Parliament would improve democratic effectiveness. Moreover the optimism expressed by the Scottish people about the role the Parliament had to play in democratic renewal was almost universal, showing no significant differences between different social groups. This chapter assesses the extent to which, in summer 2000, the Scottish people still held high expectations of their Parliament, and the extent to which people felt their expectations had been met.

In order to understand changing attitudes to the Parliament it is useful to distinguish between different clusters of attitudes. This chapter considers three such clusters. It considers first the changing attitudes of the Scottish people in terms of their expectations for democratic effectiveness, second their views on the effectiveness of the Parliament in terms of policy outcomes and finally their beliefs and preferences about the Parliament's position within the UK polity.

Before we consider these three clusters of attitudes to the Parliament it is essential to look at the overall preferences for the government of Scotland held by the Scottish people, as these provide the wider context within which any changes in attitudes towards the Parliament must be located. After the referendum of 1997 there was an upsurge of support for independence for Scotland and an increased proportion of the people of Scotland who believed independence was likely in the next twenty years (Paterson et al 2001, Chapter 6). By the time of the first elections to the Parliament, however, it was clear that a Parliament with taxation powers was by far the most popular option, with 50 per cent support. As Table 6.1 shows, this position remained almost static in the first year of operation of the Parliament. In 2000, 47 per cent of the Scottish people favoured a Parliament with taxation powers, whilst the proportion favouring independence remained at a little under one third.

Support for the Parliament with taxation powers as the preferred constitutional arrangement comes from almost all groups within Scottish society. Only two groups, Scottish National Party supporters and those who express their national identity as Scottish and not British, have Independence as the preferred option, with 78 per cent of SNP supporters preferring independence and 46 per cent of those who say they are Scottish and not British preferring independence. In all other groups, defined according to social class, age, religion, party identification, national identification, and gender (including among Conservative party supporters), the most popular arrangement is a Parliament with taxation powers. This is remarkably uniform support for the Parliament, and suggests, with the exception of the groups identified above, that there is little demand for further change in the constitutional arrangements for the government of Scotland. However, as we shall see later in the chapter, this is only true of the over-arching framework of government; there remain demands for more reform in terms of the powers of the Parliament.

In addition to this general question about constitutional preferences respondents were also asked to identify the institution they believed should have the most influence over the way Scotland is run. Again there is virtually no change between 1999 and 2000 on this measure. In 1999, 74 per cent believed the Scottish Parliament should be the most influential; this remained at 72 per cent in 2000, with other institutions such as the UK government at Westminster and local councils in Scotland receiving small minorities of support.

Table 6.1 Constitutional preferences 1997-2000

	1997	1999	2000
Independent from UK and EU	9	10	11
Independent from UK within EU	28	18	19
Elected Parliament with taxation powers	32	50	47
Elected Parliament without taxation powers	9	8	8
No elected Parliament	17	10	12
Sample size	676	1482	1663

Thus, the starting point for this chapter appears to be one of little change in people's attitudes to the Parliament: it commands majority support both as a preferred constitutional option and as the body most people in Scotland would like to see have control over how Scotland is run. On the face of it there seem to have been few changes in support for the Parliament between 1999 and 2000, but we shall see below that these high levels of support for the Parliament hide the dramatic changes that occurred in the expectations people have of it.

DEMOCRATIC EFFECTIVENESS AND THE POLITICAL SYSTEM

At the time of the referendum to establish the Scottish Parliament there was much optimism that the Parliament would reinvigorate Scottish democracy. This was in part based on the idea that 'the Parliament represents a fresh break from established British Parliamentary tradition and practice' (Smith and Gray 1999). Smith and Gray continue with a particularly pertinent question

If Parliaments elsewhere have been unable to reverse increasing dissatisfaction with the effectiveness of contemporary processes of democracy, why should the establishment of a new forum in Scotland address these same issues for the Scottish polity? (Smith and Gray 1999: 429).

In other words, is it reasonable to expect a new Parliament to revive flagging interest in Parliamentary democracy? Yet the evidence from the 1997 Referendum Study was clear: large majorities of the Scottish electorate believed that the Parliament would give Scotland a stronger voice in the UK and would give the ordinary people of Scotland more say in how the country was governed (Brown et al 1999). This section assesses whether or not that optimism was sustained over the first year of operation of the Scottish Parliament.

It is clear that democratic renewal covers a very wide range of potential changes and attitudes. Here we focus on two particular aspects of this. Respondents to the 1997 referendum survey, the 1999 Scottish Parliament Survey and the 2000 Scottish Social Attitudes Survey were each asked whether they believed that the Parliament would give Scotland a stronger voice in the UK and give ordinary people more say in how Scotland is governed. Table 6.2 shows how these measures of optimism about the Parliament changed over the 3 years between the referendum and the first year of operation.

Table 6.2 Democratic effectiveness and the Scottish Parliament

% responding Scottish Parliament will:	1997	1999	2000
Give Scotland a stronger voice in the UK	70	70	52
Give ordinary people more say in how Scotland is governed	79	64	44
Sample size	676	1482	1663

In each case it is clear that the optimism about the Parliament has waned. At the time of the referendum, clear majorities believed that the Parliament would give Scotland a stronger voice and ordinary people more say; by the time of the elections to the Parliament this had changed a little but there remained clear optimism. However, by 2000 the position had altered dramatically, with the majority of respondents believing that the Parliament would make no difference to the say that ordinary people have in how Scotland is governed and just 50 per cent believing that Scotland had a stronger voice in the UK as a result of the Parliament. It should be stressed that in a time series such as this, question wordings are not always identical. The wording of the question described a hypothetical situation in 1997 and 1999 (i.e. before the Parliament was officially established): will a Scottish Parliament give Scotland a stronger voice in the United Kingdom/give ordinary people more say in how Scotland is governed. In 2000 an assessment of a 'real' situation (a year after the Parliament began work) was called for: from what you have seen and heard so far do you think that having a Scottish Parliament is going to give Scotland a stronger voice in the United Kingdom/ordinary people more say in how Scotland is governed. In addition, this was not a complete reversal of optimism but rather a move to a greater belief that the Parliament would make no difference. Nonetheless this does not alter the fact that there have been dramatic falls in optimism about the Parliament in terms of its ability to bring about democratic renewal. This may be interpreted as people having high expectations in the abstract but finding that their experiences of the first year of the Parliament did not match up to these expectations. It is interesting to note that the two measures appear to decline at different rates. Optimism that the Parliament will give ordinary people more say seems to decline between the referendum and the elections to the Parliament as well as over the first year of the Parliament, whilst optimism about giving Scotland a stronger voice remains high between 1997 and 1999 and then declines sharply between 1999 and 2000. One reason for this may be that by 1999 the Scottish people had already experienced the first elections to the Parliament and were perhaps disappointed by the lack of 'ordinary people' who were elected to the Parliament. In this sense the idea that the Parliament would give ordinary people more say was to some extent tested earlier (at the time of the elections) than the proposition that the Parliament would give Scotland a stronger voice in the UK. It should be stressed, however, that in 1999 there remained a majority who believed that the Parliament would give ordinary people more say, but that this was a reduced majority from 1997.

One of the key characteristics of the optimism in 1997 was the remarkable degree of agreement amongst different groups within Scottish society. Thus the only group without a majority agreeing that the Parliament would give Scotland a stronger voice and ordinary people more say were those that identified with the Conservative party, itself a relatively small group. Amongst all other groups, defined according to age, sex, class, religion, national identity, and party identification, there were majorities optimistic about the difference that the Parliament would make. Within each of these groups changes in the optimism about the Parliament have occurred in similar ways to the overall trend, that is there is an overall decline in both the proportion believing the Parliament gives Scotland a stronger voice and in the proportion believing it gives ordinary people more say. Moreover, the trend identified above, whereby optimism about giving ordinary people more say falls between 1997 and 1999 whereas the fall in optimism about the Parliament giving Scotland a stronger voice occurs almost entirely between 1999 and 2000, is repeated within almost every social group. There are, however, some notable exceptions to this overall trend. Amongst Conservative party identifiers and those who asserted a predominantly British national identity, optimism about the Parliament giving Scotland a stronger voice grew between 1997 and 1999; this is likely to be a reflection of the hostility of these groups in 1997 becoming an acceptance of the Parliament by 1999, bringing them more closely in line with other groups within Scotland.

Table 6.3 shows the proportions of various social groups agreeing that the Parliament gives Scotland a stronger voice and ordinary people more say in 2000. As the table shows, differences according to party identity are largely as we might expect, with SNP supporters remaining the most optimistic, closely followed by Labour and Liberal Democrat supporters. However, differences according to age are particularly interesting as it is the youngest age group (those aged 18-30) who are most optimistic about the Parliament, with a majority of this age group expressing optimism on both measures. This is of particular interest in the light of debates about disengagement from the political process in this age group and recent turnout figures at the UK general election where less than 45 per cent of this group turned out to vote.

Table 6.3 Views of democratic effectiveness by age and by party identification

	% agreeing that the parliament will give		
	Stronger voice in UK	Ordinary people more say	Sample size
Party identification			
None	41	32	179
Conservative	37	28	269
Labour	55	49	621
Liberal Democrat	56	48	121
SNP	62	51	319
Age			
18-30	58	52	312
31-44	52	45	460
45-59	51	39	366
60+	47	40	525

A further measure of political engagement is the extent to which people believe that it matters who is in power. Respondents were asked to say how much they agreed or disagreed with the statement it doesn't matter much which party is in power, things go on much the same. While this is not a measure of attitudes to the Parliament directly it offers us a deeper understanding of whether a lack of optimism about the Parliament and democratic renewal is related to more general disillusionment with the political process. (See Chapter 7 for a more detailed analysis of attitudes towards democracy and participation.) Table 6.4 shows the way in which responses to this question changed in the period 1997-2000.

It is striking that, in 2000, 76 per cent of the Scottish people either strongly agreed or agreed that it doesn't matter which party is in power (it should also be noted that this is in line with other parts of the UK). In addition, this has increased substantially since 1997 when a little over a third agreed with the statement. This increase has occurred across the three years with changes between 1997 and 1999 as well as between 1999 and 2000. As with attitudes towards democratic effectiveness, these changes have occurred in all groups of Scottish society. The groups with the lowest proportions in agreement are the salariat and Labour party supporters, perhaps because these groups are more likely either to be in positions of power themselves or to support those who are in power. (Nonetheless a majority in these groups also agree with the statement).

Table 6.4 Doesn't much matter who is in power 1997-2000

	1997	1999	2000
Agree Strongly	8	7	20
Agree	31	48	56
Neither	14	9	6
Disagree	40	31	17
Disagree Strongly	6	4	1
Sample size	676	1482	1663

The interesting question for this chapter is the extent to which this belief that it doesn't matter who is in power goes hand in hand with a lack of optimism about the ability of the Scottish Parliament to give Scotland a stronger voice in the UK and ordinary people more say in government. In other words, are the changes in optimism a result of experiences of the Scottish Parliament or of a more general disillusionment with the political process?

Table 6.5 shows the proportion within each response to the statement it doesn't matter who is in power who believed that the Parliament would give Scotland a stronger voice and ordinary people more say. If all of these measures are representing the same underlying dimension of disillusionment then those who agree strongly that it doesn't matter who is in power should be the least optimistic about the Scottish Parliament making a difference.

Table 6.5 Democratic effectiveness and political disillusionment

| | % agreeing that the Parliament will give | | |
	Stronger voice in UK	Ordinary people more say	Sample size
Doesn't matter which party is in power			
Agree Strongly	43	49	334
Agree	53	60	926
Neither	67	65	97
Disagree	53	72	279
Disagree Strongly	59	82	21

As the table shows this relationship is far from clear-cut. There is a clear relationship between optimism about the Parliament giving ordinary people more say and whether or not it matters who is in power, but there is no clear relationship between this and optimism about giving Scotland a stronger voice. A possible explanation for this may be that these two measures of optimism about the Parliament are measuring slightly different things. Whether or not the Parliament gives ordinary people more say is more likely to be related to a general disillusionment with the political process, whereas giving Scotland a stronger voice is related to the position of Scotland within that political process. Some evidence to support this suggestion can be seen by the optimism of different party supporters. Supporters of the SNP are more likely to believe that the Parliament gives Scotland a stronger voice than supporters of Labour and the Liberal Democrats (62 per cent compared with 55 per cent) but are only slightly more likely to believe that the Parliament gives ordinary people more say (51 per cent compared with 49 per cent).

To summarise these findings, it is clear that there has been a fall in optimism about what the Parliament is likely to achieve in terms of democratic renewal. Whilst this has not been replaced by a pessimistic belief that the Parliament has made things worse, it does represent a considerable switch towards the belief that the Parliament has made no difference. As shown above, this is by no means a reflection of dissatisfaction with the idea of a Parliament, as support for the Parliament as an institution remains high. Levels of optimism have changed in similar ways amongst all social groups in Scottish society and in terms of attitudes to the Parliament there would appear to be more agreement amongst groups than differences between them (this was also true of the high levels of optimism at the time of the referendum).

THE SCOTTISH PARLIAMENT AND POLICY EXPECTATIONS

Earlier research, which looked at voting in the 1997 referendum, pointed clearly to policy expectations as the basis for the Yes-Yes vote (Brown et al 1999, Chapter 6). Support was based on high expectations that the Parliament would improve services in Scotland, in particular education and the health service. It is difficult in these areas to make direct comparisons over time. The questions asked in 1997 and 1999 are posed in the abstract and are about the expectations people held of the Parliament, whereas in 2000 the questions are more directly related to actual issues of policy and are of course more focused on what had happened during the first year of the Parliament rather than on a hypothetical future. Chapter 9 looks at the extent to which the actual policies pursued by the Scottish Executive have been in line with the centre of Scottish opinion; in this section we consider the way in which expectations of policy have changed over a rather narrower selection of broad policy areas: education, the economy and taxation. These three areas are chosen because there are comparable questions over the three surveys.

Table 6.6 shows the changes in expectations around these policy areas between 1997 and 2000. As with attitudes to democratic effectiveness, there is a fall in the expectations of the Parliament; in each case this is accompanied by an increase in people believing that the Parliament will make no difference rather than in people believing that things will get worse. Attitudes to taxation are more difficult to interpret in this context. In 1997 it was clear that increased taxation by the Parliament would not be viewed as a bad thing by the Scottish people if it was to allow for better public services (Surridge et al 1999). We cannot, therefore, straightforwardly interpret higher taxation as being a policy dislike. Indeed there remains 56 per cent of the Scottish people who believe that the

Parliament will lead to increased taxation, the only one of the three areas considered where a majority believe that the Parliament will make any difference. It is important to note that these changes occur gradually with drops between 1997 and 1999 as well as between 1999 and 2000. This suggests that changes in policy expectations are not responding directly to the actions of the Parliament as there was declining optimism about these areas even before the Parliament's first sitting. It should also be noted that the question wording for these items was changed between 1999 and 2000, in the same way as the questions about democratic effectiveness, although again this cannot be the sole cause of the changes because of the changes occurring between 1997 and 1999 when the question wording remained constant.

The fall in expectations that the Parliament will improve the standard of education in Scotland and make Scotland's economy better are dramatic, and occur both between 1997 and 1999 and between 1999 and 2000. However, it is not possible at this stage in the life of the Parliament to say whether this represents a continuing downward trend or is the result of the very high expectations of the Parliament being tempered to more realistic expectations of what the Parliament is actually able to achieve. It will be important to look at these trends over the longer term.

In order to understand how these attitudes to policy vary across groups within Scottish society we focus exclusively on attitudes towards education. This is an area that has had a great deal of publicity during the early stages of the Parliament – firstly in the coalition, which faced the issue of finance for higher education, and secondly in the handling of the problems with examination results in summer 2000 (after our present survey). Moreover it is an area of policy that is firmly in the control of the Parliament, unlike taxation and the economy, for which a large part of policy making remains a reserved power of Westminster.

Looking at differences within Scottish society, the pattern of expectations here bears a remarkable resemblance to expectations of democratic effectiveness. Changes in attitudes have occurred in almost identical ways across all social groups, with only Liberal Democrat and SNP supporters having a majority who expect the Parliament to improve the standard of education. Again these attitudes are marked by the degree of similarity among social groups rather than by differences. It is worth noting from other chapters that it is certainly not the case that there is a consensus in Scottish society around social and political attitudes. However, in terms of expectations of the Parliament and its ability to effect democratic renewal and improve education, groups within Scottish society are in agreement with each other, with roughly half of each group expecting the Parliament to make no difference.

Table 6.6 Policy expectations of the Parliament 1997-2000

	1997	1999	2000
Taxes			
A lot higher	11	10	12
A little higher	65	54	44
No different	20	26	37
A little lower	3	4	2
A lot lower	*	*	*
Sample size	657	1482	1663
Economy			
A lot better	18	6	4
A little better	46	37	32
No difference	24	37	45
A little worse	10	10	10
A lot worse	2	2	2
Sample size	657	1482	1663
Improved Education			
Yes	71	56	43
No difference	19	36	49
No	3	3	3
Sample size	676	1482	1663

THE ROLE OF THE PARLIAMENT IN THE UK POLITY

As indicated above, there is both widespread support for the Parliament amongst the Scottish people and significantly reduced expectations of what the Parliament may be able to deliver. In this section we consider attitudes towards the place of the Parliament and the powers it has, to understand how these apparently contradictory positions are held. That is, how is the support for the Parliament reconciled with lowered expectations?

Table 6.7 More powers for the Scottish Parliament

The Scottish Parliament should be given more powers	1999	2000
Agree strongly	14	23
Agree	42	43
Neither	20	15
Disagree	18	12
Disagree strongly	4	5
Sample size	1482	1663

An important factor here is whether or not the Scottish people believe that the Parliament should be given more powers. It is clear from Table 6.1 above that there is not majority support for Scottish independence, but is there support for a more powerful Parliament within the current political framework? The question of whether or not the Parliament should have more powers was asked in only 1999 and 2000; we can therefore only look at shifts in this position between 1999 and 2000, a relatively short time period. Table 6.7 shows responses to this question in each year. Over this short time period there was a growth of 10 per cent in the proportion agreeing that the Parliament should have more powers, from 56 per cent in 1999 to 66 per cent in 2000; this is especially marked in the 'strongly agree' category where we find that by 2000 almost one quarter of the Scottish people strongly agreed that the Parliament should be given more powers. This is a remarkable endorsement of the idea of a

Parliament, with two thirds of people believing that the powers of the Parliament should be increased.

It is crucial to understand the reasons that lie behind this desire for greater powers. Is it the case that people believe the Parliament is doing a good job and so should be given more powers because it has proved itself or is it that people are frustrated by the lack of achievements of the Parliament and believe it needs more powers in order to achieve the changes they would like to see in policy?

If the first scenario is correct, that is that people want the Parliament to have greater powers because they are happy with the changes it has brought about, we would expect that those who are optimistic about the Parliament in terms of democratic renewal and policy areas would be more supportive of increasing the Parliament's powers, and conversely that those who are pessimistic about the Parliament would be least likely to wish to see its powers extended. However, if the second scenario is correct we would expect those with lower expectations of the Parliament to be more in favour of increased powers (this assumes that those who are less optimistic about the Parliament still favour the Parliament as the mean to achieving those ends).

Table 6.8 Optimism about the Parliament and desire for greater powers

	% wanting Parliament to have more powers	Sample size
Stronger Voice		
Yes	77	849
No difference	57	661
No	47	103
Ordinary people		
Yes	79	725
No difference	57	840
No	58	49
Improved education		
Yes	80	707
No difference	58	826
No	43	54

The figures in Table 6.8 show that the position is not obviously one that fits into either of the scenarios described above. The desire to see a Parliament with greater powers has grown across all groups regardless of their optimism or pessimism about the Parliament. However, those with highest expectations of the Parliament remain most likely to want greater powers, but even amongst those who are most pessimistic (those who say that the Parliament has not given Scotland a stronger voice, has not improved the standard of education and has not given ordinary people more say) almost half wish to see the Parliament given more powers. It remains impossible with the survey data to disentangle the extent to which this fits with scenario one or two, but what is clear is that there remains a belief in the Parliament to deliver something even if that something is not necessarily increased democratic effectiveness or improvements in education.

Turning to differences between social groups in their desire to see the Parliament given more powers, we again find that there has been an increase amongst all social groups. However, this tendency is most marked among groups that are often seen as disaffected from the political process. For example, 80 per cent of those aged 18-30 agreed that the Parliament should be given more powers. In contrast just 40 per cent of Conservative party identifiers wish to see the Parliament given more powers. As with attitudes towards democratic effectiveness and policy expectations, it is the degree of similarity amongst groups rather than the differences between them that are most striking.

A further way of understanding the support for the Scottish Parliament is through a consideration of the trust the Scottish people have in their political institutions more generally. Is the support for the Scottish Parliament built on a bed of mistrust in other political institutions, and if so to what extent can the Parliament itself avoid this mistrust? Chapter 7 will examine many elements of trust in MPs and political institutions; in this chapter the focus is on the way in which trust in two institutions, the UK government and the Scottish Parliament, is related to support for the Parliament.

Turning first to the UK government, it is clear that the Scottish people have relatively low levels of trust in the UK government to work in Scotland's interests, with just four per cent trusting the UK government to work in Scotland's interests 'Just about always' and 53 per cent trusting the UK government 'Only some of the time' in

137

1997. However there has been a fall in trust even from the relatively low levels of 1997, to such that in 2000 just over one quarter of the Scottish people trusted the UK government 'almost never' to work in Scotland's interests. By contrast, trust in the Scottish Parliament was somewhat higher, with over 50 per cent of people trusting the Scottish Parliament just about always or most of the time. Perhaps of some concern is that this level of trust has fallen since 1997 when four fifths of the Scottish people trusted the Parliament at least most of the time. If we consider the views of these groups as to whether or not the Parliament should have greater powers, an interesting picture emerges. There is a clear relationship between trust in the UK government and a desire for the Scottish Parliament to have more powers, with the level of support for more powers for the Scottish Parliament being 54 per cent among those who trust the UK government at best most of the time. This rises to 72 per cent amongst those who trust the UK government almost never, suggesting that some of the desire to see greater powers rest with the Scottish Parliament is due to a feeling that powers will be better used in Scotland than in Westminster.

This pattern can also be seen by considering the extent to which the Scottish people feel that the present system of governing in Britain works well. (The overall responses to this question and how they relate to other elements of political trust are considered in Chapter 7.) Table 6.9 shows the proportions within each response category to the question of who wishes to see the Scottish Parliament have greater powers. It is clear from the table that those who feel that the system of government could be improved see an element of that improvement to be giving the Scottish Parliament greater powers, as 70 per cent of those who believe that the system could be improved a lot would like to see a Parliament with more power.

Further evidence that this desire for greater powers is driven by a desire for a strong Parliament can be found by considering the relationship between constitutional preferences and a desire for more powers. Table 6.10 shows how the proportions of each group who would like the Parliament to have more powers changed between 1999 and 2000.

Table 6.9 Government works well and desire for more powers

	% wanting Parliament to have more powers	Sample size
Works extremely well and could not be improved	41	19
Could be improved in small ways but mainly works well	57	517
Could be improved quite a lot	70	852
Needs a great deal of improvement	75	273

Table 6.10 Constitutional preferences and desire for more powers

	% wanting more powers			
	1999	Sample size	2000	Sample size
Independent from UK and EU	82	148	90	187
Independent from UK within EU	85	247	89	307
Parliament with taxation powers	52	753	67	779
Parliament without taxation powers	40	130	42	126
No change	15	129	21	194

It is not surprising to find that the greatest proportions wanting more powers to the Parliament are to be found amongst those who prefer independence. However, the important change that has taken place during the first year of the Parliament is a change in the views of those who support a Parliament with taxation powers as their preferred constitutional arrangement. Amongst this group in 1999 just half wished to see the Parliament given greater powers. By 2000 this had grown to 67 per cent, a change of 15 percentage points in just one year. Thus, the Parliament with taxation powers may be the 'settled will' of the Scottish people but the extent of its powers remains an issue for debate, with two thirds of those in favour of the Parliament wanting to see it given more powers.

Table 6.11 Who does and should have most influence over Scottish government

	1999	2000	Should have (2000)
Scottish Parliament	41	13	72
UK government at Westminster	39	66	13
Local councils in Scotland	8	10	10
European Union	4	4	1
Sample size	1482	1663	1663

What then is the cause of this increased desire to see more powers rest with the Scottish Parliament? Table 6.11 compares the views of the Scottish people in 1999 and in 2000 as to which institution they believe has the most influence over the way Scotland is run; it also compares this with the institutions people believed ought to have the most influence. There is a striking mismatch between the institutions the Scottish people would like to have most influence and those that they believe do in fact have most influence. As noted above, 72 per cent would like the Scottish Parliament to have the greatest influence over the way Scotland is run. However, just 13 per cent believe that in reality it is the Scottish Parliament that has the most influence, with two thirds believing that the UK government at Westminster has retained the most influence. This position has also changed over the first year of operation of the Parliament. In 1999 41 per cent of Scots believed that the Parliament would have the most influence, with 39 per cent believing it would be Westminster. This mismatch between the desires of the people and their perceptions of the real situation may account for some of the pressure for greater powers for the Parliament. If we consider the views of those who want the Scottish Parliament to be most influential, but who believe that the UK government is most influential, then we find that 80 per cent of this group would like the Parliament to have greater powers.

CONCLUSION

The chapter began by considering the changes in attitudes to the Scottish Parliament. It has shown how there is widespread support for the Parliament and that this support is amongst almost all social groups within Scotland; it is no longer strongly related to social characteristics or political allegiances (with the exception of supporters of the SNP). Whilst there has been a fall in the optimism about what the Parliament can deliver to Scotland in terms of democratic effectiveness and policy changes, this has not dampened overall support for the Parliament. Moreover, these changes in optimism have also occurred in almost all social groups within Scottish society. This suggests that attitudes towards the Parliament are now far more similar among social groups than they are different; it is no longer possible to use the social characteristics of people in Scotland to predict their attitudes to the Scottish Parliament in a way that would have been possible in previous years (Brand et al 1994, Brown et al 1999).

To turn to the question posed by the title of this volume – are social ties fragmenting? – in the case of attitudes towards the Parliament the answer is most definitely no. There are few differences in attitudes between groups, despite the much larger differences in moral, social and political attitudes discussed in other chapters. The conclusion would be that whatever the particular attitudes and preferences held by Scottish people, they believe that the Scottish Parliament will serve them best in achieving their goals.

REFERENCES

Brand, J., Mitchell, J. and Surridge, P. (1994), 'Social Constituency and ideological profile: Scottish Nationalism in the 1990's', *Political Studies* 42, pp. 616-29.

Brown, A., McCrone, D., Paterson, L. and Surridge, P. (1999), *The Scottish Electorate*, Basingstoke: Macmillan.

Brown, A., Curtice, J., Hinds, K., McCrone, D., Park, A., Paterson, L., and Surridge, P. (2001), *New Scotland, New Politics*, Edinburgh: Edinburgh University Press.

Smith, C. F. and Gray, P. (1999), 'The Scottish Parliament: [Re-]Shaping Parliamentary Democracy in the Information Age', *Parliamentary Affairs*, 52, pp. 429-41.

7

DEVOLUTION AND DEMOCRACY: NEW TRUST OR OLD CYNICISM?

JOHN CURTICE

INTRODUCTION

The Labour government elected in 1997 had a number of objectives when it created the Scottish Parliament. One was undoubtedly political calculation, a fear that unless the party was seen to deliver some form of home rule the party's electoral base north of the border might be undermined by the Scottish National Party. After all it had already suffered the occasional spectacular loss to the nationalists in parliamentary by-elections. Even worse, unless devolution was put in place Scots might decide that the UK would never accommodate their wish for more autonomy and so would resort to demanding independence instead, a development that would deny Labour all of its Scottish MPs at Westminster. On the other hand if Scotland were granted her own parliament then the nationalist genie might well be put back in the bottle and public support for the maintenance of the Union strengthened rather than weakened.

But there was another rather wider objective that applied not only to Labour's plans for devolution, but also to the whole range of proposals for constitutional reform to which it was committed when it entered office in 1997. The final years of the last Conservative administration had been characterised by growing concern about the standing of politicians and the political system in the eyes of the public across the UK, particularly as the governing party became increasingly embroiled in allegations of financial and sexual impropriety that came to be known as 'sleaze' (Crewe 1995). At the same time some commentators argued that public expectations of politics and politicians were rising and that the UK's constitution needed to adapt to a demand for increased and more varied opportunities for participation in government decision making (Dalton and Kuechler 1990; Dunleavy, Weir and Subrahmanyam 1995). In short, constitutional reform was regarded as a remedy for restoring public trust and confidence in the UK's political system.

The father of devolution, Donald Dewar, himself articulated that argument in a speech that he gave soon after Scotland had voted in favour of devolution in the September 1997 referendum. He argued:

> reform is absolutely vital if the United Kingdom is to have a chance of building the kinds of principles and system which perhaps make the public opinion polls about the standing of politicians change quite dramatically. (Dewar 1998).

And in arguing this we can reasonably assume that Mr Dewar was not anticipating that constitutional reform would lower rather than raise the standing of politicians.

This chapter examines what impact the advent of devolution appears to have had on the Scottish public's trust and confidence in the political system in its early life. Is it the case that the public in Scotland now has more trust and confidence than was the case prior to the introduction of devolution? Perhaps even more importantly is there any evidence that trust and confidence has risen more rapidly in Scotland, which now does enjoy the fruits of devolution, than it has done in England, where devolution is still largely absent? Or alternatively do we find that Mr Dewar's hopes for constitutional reform have so far at least not been realised, and that perceptions of the political system amongst Scots are still little different from their counterparts in England? Answering these questions will enable us to assess whether Scots' ties to their political system as whole have strengthened or weakened in the immediate wake of devolution.

THREE KEY MEASURES

We will address these questions using three key measures of Scots' attitudes towards their political system – political efficacy, political trust and perceptions of the need for improvement in the system of government. The first two of these have made a regular appearance in the literature on attitudes towards political systems ever since they were coined and developed by Almond and Verba in a major cross-national study of 'political culture' in the late 1950s (Almond and Verba 1963). By political efficacy we mean the degree to which the public feel that the political system is able and willing to respond to the demands that are made of it. By political trust, in contrast, we mean the degree to which the public trust politicians to take decisions that are in the national interest. In short, political efficacy refers to the degree to which the political system is able to respond to demands from 'below' while political trust refers to the extent to which political leaders are trusted to make the best decisions from 'above'. For Almond and Verba an ideal political culture was one where the public both felt that the system was reasonably efficacious and had a fair degree of trust in their political leaders, albeit not to the extent that they never questioned the wisdom of what their leaders were doing.

Our survey contained a number of questions that between them were intended to measure the level of political efficacy and trust in Scotland in the immediate wake of devolution. Some of them indeed are items that were included in Almond and Verba's original study. Most importantly for our purposes many of them are items that were also previously administered in Scotland prior to the creation of the Scottish Parliament and at the same time have also been asked on a regular basis in recent years throughout Great Britain on the British Social Attitudes Survey.

In order to measure political efficacy we asked respondents the extent to which they agreed or disagreed with three propositions. These were:

Generally speaking those we elect as MPs lose touch with people pretty quickly.

Parties are only interested in people's votes, not in their opinions.

It doesn't really matter which party is in power, in the end things go on pretty much the same.

For the most part in this chapter we combine the responses to these three items into a single scale measure of political efficacy. This scale ranges from a score of 1, that is those with very low efficacy, to one of 4, that is those with very high efficacy.[1]

Meanwhile we aimed to tap the degree to which respondents had trust in the political system by asking four questions. These are:

How much do you trust British governments of any party to place the needs of the nation above the interests of their own political party?

And how much do you trust the politicians of any party in Britain to tell the truth when they are in a tight corner?

How much do you trust the UK government to work in Scotland's best long-term interest?

How much do you trust the Scottish Parliament to work in Scotland's best interest?

In each case respondents were offered a choice of 'just about always', 'most of the time', 'only some of the time' or 'almost never'. It might be thought that the latter two items would be tapping feelings of nationalism and attitudes towards the Union rather than trust more generally, but in fact we find that those who, for example, say that they trust politicians of any party to tell the truth are also more likely to say they trust both the Scottish Parliament and the UK government to work in Scotland's interests. This means that we can also construct a scale of political trust from all four of these items. This scale has three categories, low, medium and high.[2]

Our third measure also has a venerable history if a slightly shorter one. It was first asked by the Royal Commission on the Constitution chaired by Lord Kilbrandon between 1969-73, a commission that was established by the then Labour government in response to the first electoral success of Scottish and Welsh nationalists in 1966 and 1967 (Crowther-Hunt and Peacock 1973). For our purposes, of more immediate importance is the fact that it has been asked on a number of occasions in recent years in Scotland. The question simply taps the degree to which people feel the current method of running government in Britain is satisfactory or rather is in need of improvement. It asks:

Which of these statements best describes your opinion of the present system of governing Britain?

It works extremely well and could not be improved.

It could be improved in small ways but mainly works well.

It could be improved quite a lot.

It needs a great deal of improvement.

These then are the measures that we use in this chapter to assess whether public trust and confidence in the political system has risen or fallen in the wake of the creation of the Scottish Parliament. If we are to argue that Donald Dewar's aspirations were fulfilled then we should be able to show that political efficacy and political trust in Scotland have increased. We should also be able to show that the proportion who believe that the system of governing Britain needs little or no improvement has fallen.

RECENT TRENDS IN TRUST AND CONFIDENCE

There is little doubt that Donald Dewar was right in believing that trust and confidence in politicians was in need of improvement. Certainly, the British Social Attitudes survey, which as we have already noted has asked these items on a regular basis in recent years, found that trust and confidence in the political system declined during the final years of the last UK Conservative government across Britain as a whole. Trust in government and political efficacy both fell, while there was an increase in the proportion that felt that the system of government needed improvement. The one more hopeful indication was that there were signs that the election of a new government in 1997 may have done something to help reverse those trends (Curtice and Jowell 1997).

But, alas for Mr Dewar's vision, there is little sign that creating the Scottish Parliament has so far at least done much to restore trust and confidence. Rather, on all three of our measures the reverse appears to have happened. In Table 7.1, for example, we show the proportion of people who agreed with the three statements that comprise our political efficacy scale. The recovery in political efficacy that, according to Britain-wide data at least, occurred after the general election has not been sustained. Efficacy was already lower in 1999 immediately after the first Scottish Parliament election than it had been after the September 1997 referendum. Moreover, efficacy fell even further during the first twelve months of the Scottish Parliament's existence. So, for example, whereas in 1997 only around two in five agreed that parties were only interested in people's votes, by the time of our most recent survey nearly three quarters took that view.

Table 7.1 Recent trends in political efficacy

per cent agree	1997		1999	2000
	General Election	Referendum		
MPs lose touch	na	60	66	72
Parties only interested in votes	64	58	65	73
Doesn't matter who in power	42	40	55	75
Sample size	841	676	1427	1663

na = not asked.

Sources: Scottish Election Study 1997; Scottish Referendum Study 1997; Scottish Parliament Election Study/Scottish Social Attitudes Survey 1999; Scottish Social Attitudes Survey 2000

A similar picture emerges when we look at our measures of political trust. In each case the proportion that almost never trusts the body or group in question has risen since the question was first asked either after the May 1997 general election or else the September 1997 referendum. It would appear that the institution that has lost most trust is the British government. Only one in ten almost never trusted British governments to put the interests of the nation first in 1997. Now a little over one quarter take that view. Meanwhile there has been an almost identical trend in the proportion who never trust the UK government to work in Scotland's interest. However, while trust in the Scottish Parliament is clearly much higher than it is in the UK government, even that in fact has fallen. Whereas at the time of the referendum no fewer than 83 per cent trusted the parliament to work in Scotland's interest 'just about always' or 'most of the time', only just over a half do so now.

Table 7.2 Recent trends in political trust

per cent almost never trust	1997		1999	2000
	General Election	Referendum		
Governments to put nation before party	11	na	na	27
Politicians to tell the truth	42	na	na	50
UK government to work in Scotland's interests	na	11	14	26
Scottish Parliament to work in Scotland's interests	na	3	2	9
Sample size	841	676	1427	1663

na = not asked

Sources: Scottish Election Study 1997; Scottish Referendum Study 1997; Scottish Parliament Election Study/Scottish Social Attitudes Survey 1999; Scottish Social Attitudes Survey 2000

Table 7.3 Recent trends in attitudes towards system of governing Britain

per cent saying	1997	1999	2000
Could not be improved	3	1	1
Could be improved in small ways	45	43	31
Could be improved a lot	39	45	50
Needs a great deal of improvement	8	9	16
Sample size	841	1427	1663

Sources: Scottish Election Study 1997; Scottish Parliament Election Study/Scottish Social Attitudes Survey 1999; Scottish Social Attitudes Survey 2000

Meanwhile as Table 7.3 shows, the proportion believing that the system of governing Britain does not need improvement other than in small ways has fallen from nearly a half at the time of the 1997 general election to less than one in three now. Evidently Labour's extensive programme of constitutional reform has, so far at least, done little to persuade Scots that they are being governed better. Rather, the opposite appears to be the case.

PERCEPTIONS OF CONSTITUTIONAL REFORM

These findings clearly raise questions about how Scots regard the government's programme of constitutional reform now that much of it has been put in place. Perhaps in practice they have found that it does not improve the way they are being governed. Maybe, indeed, given our findings so far, they think that it has made matters worse.

Table 7.4 Perceptions of constitutional reform

by	per cent saying way Britain as a whole is governed has been		
	Improved	No Difference	Made Worse
Creating Scottish Parliament	35	44	10
Introducing freedom of information	27	56	5
Creating Welsh Assembly	18	46	4
Reforming House of Lords	8	75	6

Sample size = 1663

Source: Scottish Social Attitudes Survey 2000

In fact that last statement at least is not true. Our survey asked respondents about the contribution that they felt four of the reforms introduced by the Labour government had made to the system of governing Britain as a whole. These reforms were creating a Scottish Parliament, creating a Welsh Assembly, introducing freedom of information, and reforming the House of Lords. Only small minorities of Scots felt that any of these had actually made the way that Britain is governed worse. Thus even when it comes to the reform about which Scots are unsurprisingly most likely to have a view, that is creating the Scottish Parliament, just one in ten think that the Parliament has made things worse.

But on the other hand relatively few Scots believe that any of these reforms have improved matters either. Even creating the Scottish Parliament is only thought to have improved the way Britain is governed by just over one third. Meanwhile, so far as the other three reforms are concerned a majority simply believe that they have not made any difference, a figure that rises to no less than three quarters in respect of reform of the House of Lords.

Table 7.5 Efficacy and trust by expectations of the Scottish Parliament

| | Level of Efficacy | | | | |
	Very Low	Low	High	Very High	Sample size
Scots Parliament going to:-					
Give Scots more say in govt.	12	47	33	8	725
No difference	24	52	22	3	840
Stronger voice in UK	15	51	29	6	849
No difference	24	50	23	3	661
Increase standard of education	12	51	30	7	707
No difference	24	50	23	3	826

| | Level of Trust | | |
	Low	Medium	High
Scots Parliament going to:-			
Give Scots more say in govt.	13	73	14	723
No difference	27	62	11	837
Scotland stronger voice in UK	15	72	13	847
No difference	28	62	10	658
Increase standard of education	14	71	16	704
No difference	27	64	10	824

Source: Scottish Social Attitudes Survey 2000

So perhaps the reason why the introduction of constitutional reform in general and creating the Scottish Parliament in particular have so far failed to increase trust and confidence in government is that they have simply failed to live up to expectations. Perhaps Scots expected the Scottish Parliament to make a significant improvement, but have come to the view that in practice it has made little difference. Certainly as Paula Surridge shows in Chapter 6, Scots' expectations of what the Scottish Parliament is likely to deliver have fallen dramatically since the 1997 referendum. They are, for example, now far less likely to believe that it will increase Scotland's voice in the UK or the voice of ordinary Scots in how Scotland itself is governed. They are also now much more doubtful about whether it will improve Scotland's educational system or its economy.

Moreover, we can also demonstrate that perceptions of what impact the Scottish Parliament is likely to make are related to how efficacious and trustful Scots feel about their political system. As Table 7.5 demonstrates, those who still have high expectations of the Scottish Parliament are more likely to have a high level of political efficacy and to have trust in their political system.

For example, amongst those who believe that having a Scottish Parliament is going to give ordinary people more say in how they are governed, only around one in eight have a very low level of political efficacy or a low level of political trust. In contrast, amongst those who believe that having a Scottish Parliament is not going to make any difference, around a quarter have a very low level of efficacy or a low level of trust. The results are similar when we look at how efficacy and trust varies according to some of the other expectations of the Scottish Parliament that our survey covered.

So, expectations of the Scottish Parliament have fallen. Meanwhile, such expectations are clearly related to the level of trust and confidence Scots have in their political system. So it seems quite reasonable to suppose that the reason why trust and confidence have fallen in the immediate wake of the implementation of devolution is because the Scottish Parliament has failed to live up to expectations.

TRENDS IN TRUST AND EXPECTATIONS OF THE SCOTTISH PARLIAMENT

However if this supposition were correct we should also find one further pattern. This is that if we look at the relationship between trust and expectations of the Scottish Parliament, or alternatively between efficacy and expectations, we should find that, for those with any given set of expectations, the level of trust and efficacy now should be much the same as it was previously. Thus, for example, we should find that the level of efficacy amongst those who think that the Scottish Parliament is going to give ordinary people more say in how they are governed should be much the same now as it was in 1997 or 1999. In that event, then, the reason why trust and confidence has declined amongst Scots as a whole would be that there are now simply fewer people with high expectations of the Parliament. If on the other hand we find that the level of efficacy has fallen amongst those with high expectations, and has done so indeed as much as it has amongst those with lower expectations, then, whatever is responsible for the decline in trust and confidence, it cannot be the fall in expectations of the Scottish Parliament.

Table 7.6 examines which of these arguments are correct so far as political efficacy is concerned. It is quite clear that the decline in efficacy has not been occasioned by the decline in expectations of the Scottish Parliament. The level of political efficacy has declined both amongst those who have high expectations of the Parliament and those who do not. Indeed, if anything, efficacy has fallen most amongst those who still have high expectations. Thus, for example, there has been a 21 point increase in the incidence of low or very low efficacy amongst those who expect the Scottish Parliament to give ordinary people more say compared with a 13 point increase amongst those who do not think it would make any difference. Similar analysis of the trends in trust (not shown) produces an identical finding.

COMPARING SCOTLAND AND ENGLAND

Moreover, if falling expectations of the Scottish Parliament were responsible for the decline in efficacy we would probably also expect to observe another pattern. This is that the decline in trust and confidence has been greater in Scotland than it has in England, if indeed any decline has occurred south of the border at all. After all, England has not had any devolution that might have disappointed. If, on the other hand, we find that trust and confidence have fallen in England in much the same manner as they have in Scotland, then it would seem unlikely that the reason for that fall is any development particular to Scotland. Rather it would seem more plausible to argue that trust and confidence in the political system has been subject to similar adverse forces north and south of the border.

Table 7.6 Trends in efficacy and expectations of the Scottish Parliament

	per cent with very low or low efficacy			
	1997	1999	2000	Change 97-00
Scots Parliament going to:-				
Give Scots more say in govt.	38	47	59	+21
No difference	62	60	75	+13
Scotland stronger voice in UK	48	48	65	+17
No difference	62	62	74	+12
Increase standard of education	45	71	63	+18
No difference	60	64	74	+14

Sample sizes:			
	1997	1999	2000
Scots Parliament going to:-			
Give Scots more say in govt.	500	946	725
No difference	117	469	840
Scotland stronger voice in UK	456	1030	849
No difference	102	309	661
Increase standard of education	459	821	707
No difference	127	528	826

Sources: Scottish Referendum Study 1997; Scottish Parliament Election Study/Scottish Social Attitudes Survey 1999; Scottish Social Attitudes Survey 2000

Table 7.7 Trends in efficacy, trust and attitudes towards government in England and Scotland

per cent agree	1997	2000	Change 97-00
Parties only interested in votes			
England	62	75	+13
Scotland	64	73	+11
Doesn't matter who in power			
England	44	71	+27
Scotland	42	75	+33
per cent trust almost never			
Governments to put nation before party			
England	12	23	+11
Scotland	11	27	+16
Politicians to tell the truth			
England	42	45	+3
Scotland	42	50	+8
per cent saying system of governing Britain could be improved quite a lot/a great deal			
England	41	61	+20
Scotland	47	66	+19
Sample size			
England	2637/3150*	1928	
Scotland	841	1663	

The smaller figure applies to the first two items in the table, the larger to the last three.

Sources: British Election Study 1997; British Social Attitudes Survey 2000; Scottish Election Study 1997; Scottish Social Attitudes Survey 2000.

Table 7.7 reveals that the decline and trust in confidence that has taken place in Scotland since 1997 has indeed been matched by a similar trend in England. Not only that, but the levels of trust and confidence in the two parts of the United Kingdom have been and remain very similar to each other. Thus, for example, just after the 1997 UK General Election, in both England and Scotland, just under two thirds agreed that parties are only interested in people's votes, not their opinions, while in our latest survey the figure has increased in both countries to around three quarters. Equally, in 1997, only just over one in ten in both England and Scotland almost never trusted government to put the interests of the nation ahead of that of party. Now the figure in both places is around one in four.

Of course we should bear in mind our earlier observation that levels of trust and confidence rose across Britain as a whole just after 1997. So in both countries we are comparing the position now with a relative high point. However, if we look at the longer time series that is available to us on many of these questions across Britain as a whole we discover that levels of trust and confidence now are at least as low as they were in the mid-1990s when the last Conservative government was at its most unpopular and the allegations about sleaze were at their height (Bromley, Curtice and Seyd forthcoming). In short, the decline in trust and confidence does not appear simply to be an artefact of the period over which we have made our comparison. Rather it looks as though trust and confidence in the political system in Scotland is at or near an all time low, just as it is across the United Kingdom as a whole.

IMPLICATIONS

Donald Dewar was clearly correct, then, in believing that the standing of politicians and indeed of the political system more generally is a subject of concern. But what is now in doubt according to our evidence is his belief that constitutional reform in general or creating a Scottish Parliament in particular was the solution. So far at least, most Scots believe that these reforms have simply made little or no difference to the quality of government in Britain. As a result they have been unable to stem an apparently relentlessly receding tide in the level of trust and confidence in Britain's political system.

None of this of course demonstrates that creating the Scottish Parliament has had an adverse effect on trust and confidence. As we have seen, while expectations of that body have declined, that decline does not appear to be responsible for the fall in trust and confidence. Rather the crucial lesson from our analysis appears to be that Scotland's new political institutions have, so far at least, not been sufficiently significant or important enough in the minds of Scots to have stopped what appears to be a Britain-wide decline in trust and confidence from occurring north of the border as well. If devolution is designed to make a difference, then, so far as trust and confidence in government is concerned, it evidently still has to make an impact.

Table 7.8 Efficacy and turnout in the 1999 Scottish Parliament Election

Level of Efficacy	per cent voted in 1999 election	Sample size
Very Low	66	131
Low	69	650
High	74	526
Very High	85	174

Source: Scottish Parliamentary Election Study/Scottish Social Attitudes Survey 1999.

At the same time, however, the decline in trust and confidence could well have important and potentially deleterious implications for Scotland's new institutions. For, as Table 7.8 shows, those with low levels of trust and confidence are less likely to vote, including in elections to the Scottish Parliament (see also Paterson et al 2001). Of those with very low levels of efficacy at the time of the 1999 Scottish Parliament election, just two thirds reported voting in that election whereas amongst those with very high levels of efficacy no less than 85 per cent did so.[3] So, other things being equal, the lower the level of efficacy, the lower the likely level of turnout in Scottish Parliament elections. The decline in efficacy that, as we have seen in Table 7.1, had already occurred by 1999 may well have been one of the reasons why turnout in the first Scottish Parliamentary election was somewhat lower than many of the advocates of devolution had hoped. The further drop in efficacy between 1999 and 2000 will have done nothing to improve the prospects for a higher turnout in the next Scottish Parliamentary election in 2003. After all, the

Westminster Parliament has already seen turnout in its 2001 election fall to the lowest level since 1918.

ON A BRIGHTER NOTE?

The downturn in trust and confidence amongst Scots in their political system, despite the advent of constitutional reform, suggests that perhaps there are deeper forces at work undermining trust that such reform is doing little or nothing to check. After all, concern about an apparent decline in trust and confidence is hardly confined to the UK (Klingemann and Fuchs 1995; Norris 1999). As a result there is also no shortage of theories that aim to explain why a decline in trust and confidence might be occurring across the mature democracies.

One such argument has been popularised by Putnam (Putnam 2000)). This argues that social changes such as the rise in television viewing, the advent of two career families and suburbanisation have served to reduce the amount of time that people spend together in voluntary and social activities and that, as a result, the degree to which people trust each other has declined (see also Chapter 2). And if we are less inclined to trust each other then it would perhaps not be much of a surprise to discover that we are less inclined to trust our politicians too.

There is indeed some relationship between social and political trust, and indeed an even clearer one with political efficacy. In our survey we asked our respondents a question about social trust that has regularly appeared in the US General Social Survey and forms an important piece of evidence in Putnam's argument. Respondents were asked, 'Generally speaking, would you say most people can be trusted, or that you can't be too careful in dealing with people?'. As is reported in Chapter 2, just over half of Scots give the latter response and just under half the former. But what matters here is that those who gave the latter answer are a little more distrustful of politicians and the political system than are those who gave the former answer. Of those who say you cannot be too careful in dealing with people, 23 per cent evince low levels of trust compared with 19 per cent amongst those who say that most people can be trusted. Meanwhile, as many as 37 per cent of the former group have a high or very high level of efficacy compared with just 27 per cent of the latter.

But, even so, these differences are sufficiently small that it would take a very large decline in the level of social trust to bring about anything other than a marginal fall in the level of political trust or efficacy.[4] In any event, so far as Britain as a whole is concerned, there is no consistent evidence that the level of social trust has declined in recent years (Johnston and Jowell forthcoming). Given that, as Chapter 2 shows, the level of social trust in Scotland is currently similar to that in England, there seems little reason to anticipate that there has been any decline recently north of the border either.

Another theory that appears to have potential implications for the level of political efficacy and trust is the theory of postmaterialism developed by Inglehart (Inglehart 1977; Inglehart 1997). This argues that the relatively high and persistent affluence enjoyed by western democracies since 1945 has affected people's priorities. Instead of being primarily concerned about their material security, which it would appear they can now take for granted, they are more concerned about the opportunities for being able to express themselves. And while those who are looking to express themselves may have a high level of confidence in their own ability to make demands of the political system, their relatively high expectations of that system may also mean that they do not have much confidence in its ability to respond to their demands, let alone make them inclined to trust politicians to put the national interest first.

Inglehart dubs the new set of priorities that people allegedly have postmaterialism. In order to ascertain the level of support for postmaterialism we asked our respondents a question that has been widely used as a simple means of distinguishing postmaterialists from materialists. It runs:

Which do you think should be Britain's highest priority, the most important thing it should do?

Maintain order in the nation.

Give people more say in government decisions.

Fight rising prices.

Protect freedom of speech.

159

And which one do you think should be Britain's next highest priority, the second most important thing it should do?

Materialists are classified as those who choose the first and third options as their first and second priority, while postmaterialists are those who chose the second and fourth. Those who select any other mixture are regarded as having a mixture of materialist and postmaterialist priorities.

Table 7.9 Efficacy and postmaterialism

	Level of efficacy				
	Very Low	Low	High	Very High	Sample size
Postmaterialist	19	38	35	9	180
Mixed	14	45	33	8	787
Materialist	16	49	25	10	310

Source: Scottish Social Attitudes Survey 2000

However the reasoning as to why postmaterialism might have an impact on trust and confidence in the political system is not really supported by the evidence. As Table 7.9 shows, postmaterialists, who in any event only comprise 13 per cent of Scots, do not clearly have a lower level of efficacy than those who are materialist. Indeed, whereas 44 per cent of postmaterialists have a high or a very high level of efficacy, only 35 per cent of materialists have likewise. So here also it does not appear that we can argue that Scotland's political system is being undermined by a social change that constitutional reform is doing little or nothing to alter.

There is however one change to which we can point as a reason why Scots may be becoming less trustful of their politicians. One well-documented trend that has occurred amongst the electorate is that fewer now identify strongly with a political party (Crewe and Thomson 1999; Dalton and Wattenberg 2000). It has been argued that one of the consequences of voters having a strong party identity is not only that they support the party with which they identify at the ballot box but also that they support the political system in which that political party is a participant (Barry 1970; Crewe, Särlvik and Alt 1977). As a result strong party identifiers are more likely to believe that the system is efficacious or indeed that they can trust their politicians. Thus it is argued that any decline in party identification is likely to result in a decline in efficacy and trust.

Table 7.10 Efficacy and party identification

Strength of party identification	Level of efficacy				
	Very Low	Low	High	Very High	Sample size
Very Strong	10	38	38	15	92
Fairly Strong	11	43	32	14	449
Not very strong	15	45	33	8	808
Not an identifier	21	53	19	7	179

Source: Scottish Social Attitudes Survey 2000

Our survey confirms that party identification in Scotland is indeed as low now as it is south of the border. Only 31 per cent say they identify with a party either very or fairly strongly, the same proportion as in England. Moreover, we can also see in Table 7.10 that those who do not identify strongly with a party are less likely to have a high level of efficacy. For example, amongst the one in ten or so Scots who do not identify with a party at all, only around one in four have a high level of political efficacy, whereas over half of the small minority of very strong identifiers do so. So the low level of party identification in Scotland could indeed be contributing to the low level of trust and confidence.

However, while the decline of party identification may well be part of the reason why trust and confidence in government in Scotland has declined, it is far from a sufficient explanation. Analysis of the much longer time series available to us in the British Social Attitudes Survey reveals that trust and confidence have not simply declined in line with the decline in the level of party identification. Rather, even those who are still strong identifiers have less trust and confidence now than they did in the 1980s (Bromley, Curtice and Seyd forthcoming).

Indeed the speed of some of the changes in the level of trust and confidence that we have seen in this chapter has simply been too rapid for it to be likely that long term social change could be the sole explanation. Social change alone is never likely to explain why, for example, in 1997 around one half of Scots felt that the British system of government needed little improvement whereas three years later only around one third took that view. Scots were evidently responding to events and more immediate political circumstances over that period, even if they were not doing so in the way that Donald Dewar had hoped that they would.

CONCLUSION

Constitutional reform was meant to help develop a new bond of trust between Scotland and her politicians. In that objective at least it has so far not succeeded. Rather, old cynicism simply appears to have reached new levels. Compared with 1997 when Labour first came to office, Scots are less likely to think that their political system can respond to the demands they make of it, less willing to trust politicians and political institutions to make the right decisions, and more likely to think that Britain's system of government is in need of improvement. Scots' ties to their political system at least seem to have been fragmenting.

In this there appears to be an important implication for students of devolution. The findings in this chapter suggest it may not be so easy for devolution to make a difference as some have hoped and others feared. For while changing expectations about the Scottish Parliament might not be responsible for the recent decline in trust and confidence in the political system, the creation of the Scottish Parliament has not been sufficient to stop an apparent Britain-wide tide of increasing cynicism occurring north of the border either. Given the apparent inability of any of the social changes we have examined to account for the decline of trust and confidence either, it may well be that we have to conclude that responsibility for the decline lies with political developments at Westminster. If that is so, it is an indication that Scotland still takes considerable notice of what is going on at Westminster even though she now has her own parliament. To that degree at least Scotland's ties with the rest of the UK still appear to be very much intact.

ACKNOWLEDGEMENT

The collection of much of the data in England reported in this chapter was financed by the Economic and Social Research Council as part of its Democracy and Participation research programme (grant no. L215252032). The author is grateful to his fellow grantholders, Catherine Bromley, Roger Jowell and Ben Seyd for their support.

REFERENCES

Almond, G. and Verba, S. (1963), *The Civic Culture: Political Attitudes and Democracy in Five Nations*, Princeton, NJ: Princeton University Press.

Barry, B., (1970), *Sociologists, Economists and Democracy*, London: Macmillan.

Bromley, C., Curtice, J. and Seyd, B. (forthcoming), 'Still sceptical? Trust in government and constitutional reform', in A. Park, J. Curtice, K. Thomson, L. Jarvis, and C. Bromley (eds), *British Social Attitudes: the 18th report*, London: Sage.

Crowther-Hunt, Lord and Peacock, A. (1973), *Royal Commission on the Constitution 1969-73: Volume 2: Memorandum of Dissent*, London: HMSO.

Crewe, I. (1995), 'Oral evidence', in Nolan, chmn., *Standards in Public Life: First report of the Committee on Standards in Public Life: Transcripts of Evidence*, Cm. 2850-II, London: HMSO.

Crewe, I., Särlvik, B, and Alt, J. (1977), 'Partisan dealignment in Britain 1964-74', *British Journal of Political Science*, 7, pp. 129-90.

Crewe, I. and Thomson, K. (1999), 'Party Loyalties: Dealignment or Realignment?, in G. Evans and P. Norris (eds), *Critical Elections: British Parties and Voters in Long-Term Perspective*, London: Sage, pp. 64-86.

Curtice, J. and Jowell, R. (1997), 'Trust in the Political System', in R. Jowell. J. Curtice, A. Park, L. Brook, K. Thomson and C. Bryson (eds), *British Social Attitudes; the 14th report: The end of Conservative values?*, Aldershot: Ashgate, pp. 89-109.

Dalton, R. and Kuechler, M. (1990), *Challenging the Political Order: New Social and Political Movements in Western Democracies*, Oxford: Oxford University Press.

Dalton, R., and Wattenberg, M. (2000), *Parties without Partisans: Political Change in Advanced Industrial Democracies*, Oxford: Oxford University Press.

Dewar, D. (1998), 'The Scottish Parliament', *Scottish Affairs: Special Issue on Understanding Political Change*, pp. 4-12.

Dunleavy, P., Weir, S. and Subrahmanyam, G. (1995), 'Public Response and Constitutional Significance', *Parliamentary Affairs*, 50, pp. 733-49.

Inglehart, R. (1977), *The Silent Revolution: Changing Values and Political Styles amongst Western Publics*, Princeton: Princeton University Press.

Inglehart, R. (1997), *From Modernization to Post-Modernization: Cultural, Economic and Political Change in 43 Societies*, Princeton: Princeton University Press.

Johnston, M. and Jowell, R. (forthcoming), 'Social Capital and Social Trust', in A. Park, J. Curtice, K. Thomson, L. Jarvis, and C. Bromley (eds), *British Social Attitudes: the 18th report*, London: Sage.

Klingemann, H-D., and Fuchs, D. (eds) (1995), *Citizens and the State*, Oxford: Oxford University Press.

Norris, P. (ed.) (1999), *Critical Citizens: Global Support for Democratic Governance*, Oxford: Oxford University Press.

Putnam, R. (2000), *Bowling Alone: The Collapse and Revival of American Community*, New York: Simon and Schuster.

Swaddle, K. and Heath, A. (1989), 'Official and Reported Turnout in the British General Elections of 1987', *British Journal of Political Science* 19, pp. 537-70.

---

[1] The scale is constructed by adding up the respondent's scores for each item (which range from 1 = strongly agree to 5 = strongly disagree) dividing by the total number of items, and then rounding the result to the nearest integer. As this procedure produced only one case with a score of 5, those with a score of 4 or 5 were combined into a single category. The reliability of this scale as measured by Cronbach's alpha is 0.68. A further political efficacy item, *MPs don't care much about what people like me think*, was also included in the 2000 survey but as it had not previously been administered to a Scotland-only sample it has been excluded from the analysis reported in this chapter. Its inclusion in the scale for 2000 has no impact on the substantive conclusions that are drawn in this chapter.

[2] The scale is constructed in an analogous manner to the efficacy scale, with the two categories with the highest levels of trust being combined together. The Cronbach's alpha for the four item scale is 0.71.

[3] Observant readers will notice that the overall level of turnout implied by these figures is significantly higher than the 58 per cent of the registered electorate who actually voted in May 1999. This is a common finding in surveys and reflects a number of factors including over-reporting of having voted, a tendency for those who voted to be more likely to participate in surveys, and inaccuracies in the electoral register (Swaddle and Heath 1989). However, none of this necessarily invalidates comparisons of the level of turnout between different kinds of voters in our survey.

[4] Indeed, the relationship between social and political trust appears to be even weaker in Scotland than it is in Britain as a whole. In Scotland, 15 per cent of those who say most people can be trusted also trust governments to put the interests of the nation above that of their own party 'just about always' or 'most of the time' just two points above the equivalent figure for those who say that you cannot be too careful in dealing with people. In Britain as a whole, the gap is seven points.

8

A NATION OF REGIONS?

CATHERINE BROMLEY AND DAVID MCCRONE

INTRODUCTION

We begin our journey through the attitudes and values of Scotland's regions by turning back the clock by more than a century. Robert Louis Stevenson wrote in *The Silverado Squatters* (1895):

> Scotland is indefinable; it has no unity except upon the map. Two languages, many dialects, innumerable forms of piety, and countless local patriotisms and prejudices part us among ourselves more widely than the extreme east or west of that great continent of America. When I am at home, I feel a man from Glasgow to be something like a rival, a man from Barra to be more than half a foreigner. Yet let us meet in some far country, and whether we hail from the braes of Manor or the braes of Mar, some ready-made affection joins us on the instant. It is not race. Look at us. One is Norse, one Celtic, and another Saxon. It is not community of tongue. We have it, almost to perfection, with English, or Irish, or American. It is no tie of faith, for we detest each other's errors. And yet somewhere, deep down in the heart of each one of us, something yearns for the old land and the old kindly people. (Stevenson, R. L. 1895: 48-9).

Stevenson was drawing attention to the internal diversity of Scotland, which had long been a feature of its history. The Scottish

Crown in the Middle Ages, for example, had a particular role in holding a linguistically and ethnically diverse country together, first as loyalty to the monarch, and then to the integrity of the territory over which they ruled (Smout 1994). It had long been assumed that Scotland had fissiparous tendencies which threatened to pit region against region.

In modern times, Scotland's regional cultures remain identifiably reflected in the local press and media, which remain firmly 'regional', and associated with the catchment areas of the main towns and cities which they serve. Thus, television, radio, and the morning and evening newspapers are both reflections of, as well as means of amplifying, regional differences in Scotland. In many respects Scotland is unusually distinct within Great Britain in having a regionalised print media, as both *The Herald* and *The Scotsman* largely serve west and east Scotland respectively, in addition to the Aberdeen *Press and Journal*, and the *Dundee Courier*.

Such regional diversity was a metaphor for divergence and difference over the last twenty-five or so years in the context of growing demands for Home Rule. Opponents played the 'regional' card, reflected in the outcome of the 1979 referendum in which some regions, notably the Northern Isles, and the Border counties (but not the Highlands, and the Western Isles) voted No by clear majorities (see Table 8.1). Thus, opponents of Home Rule resorted to arguments about 'central belt' rule, the bogeymen of 'Strathclyde councillors' and 'Edinburgh lawyers' to divide north from south, Highland from Lowland, east from west. Tom Nairn caricatured this position with appropriate irony: 'Scotland? Which Scotland? – Highland or Lowland, Hugh Macdiarmid or the Sunday Post?: Scotland: if that word means anything – which I doubt – then surely it means different things in Grampian and Clydebank?'. Nairn added: 'Scotland's internal contrasts (actually no greater than in most other nations) are thus weirdly elevated into mountain ranges of peculiarity – barriers of all possible consensus and common interest' (Nairn 1997: 185)

Indeed, if we compare the results of the two referenda on devolution on a regional basis, we find interesting similarities as well as differences (Table 8.1). Thus, while all regions were voting 'yes' to the principle of a Scottish Parliament in 1997, the differentials, especially in answers to the tax-varying question (q2), reflected varying degrees of enthusiasm in different regions of Scotland.

Interestingly, it is also the case that the regional variations in the referendum vote of 1997 mirrored, to a large extent, the regional differences that were evident in 1979.

Table 8.1 Referendum results by region 1979 and 1997

% voting yes in	1979	1997 (q1)	1997 (q2)
Highlands and Islands			
Western Isles	55.8	79.4	68.4
Highland	51.0	72.6	62.1
Orkney	27.9	57.3	47.4
Shetland	27.1	62.4	51.6
North East			
Tayside	49.5	67.6	57.0
Grampian	48.3	67.6	55.6
East Central			
Fife	53.7	76.1	64.7
Lothian	50.1	74.5	63.7
Central	54.7	76.3	65.9
West Central			
Strathclyde	54.0	78.1	67.7
Borders			
Borders	40.3	62.8	50.7
Dumfries & Gall.	40.3	60.7	48.8
Scotland	51.6	74.3	63.5

Source: Pattie et al 1998

Two years after the first democratic parliament was established, it seems appropriate to explore the extent to which regional variation matters in 21st century Scotland with regard to political, social and moral issues. After all, as the parliament beds down, and 'normal' politics emerge, it is important to examine whether diversity is leading to divergence; whether Scotland is developing a regional politics in the new context of Home Rule.

METHODOLOGY

We have described Scotland's regions in fairly common-sense terms, and this map groups the constituencies into five: Highlands and Islands, North East, East Central, West Central, and Borders. We have kept the two 'rural' regions – Highlands and Islands, and Borders – apart, even though the sample numbers are quite small, although for some purposes – where they do not differ from year to year – we have amalgamated them. However, because we are using the constituency boundaries that have been in operation since 1997, we are able to treat, where appropriate, the 1999 and 2000 surveys as one, thus enhancing sample sizes.

There are some methodological issues we ought to bear in mind in dealing with geographical aggregates of this kind. Put simply, how sociologically 'real' are regions? In other words, might differences that we uncover be the outcomes of social aggregates? Thus, we know that the Borders has a disproportionate number of older people, and, like West Central Scotland, more working class people. To what extent are the regional differences we find the result of the social and demographic characteristics? In other words, are regions simply artefacts of these social differences? This is an argument we have to take seriously, and, where appropriate, we have used statistical models to see whether or not 'region' has a significant effect, independent of other relevant social factors which must be taken into account.

It is, however, important to bear in mind that while it is perfectly proper to try to identify whether differences remain once we have controlled for social variables such as age, social class and so on, we should not dismiss such differences out of hand. Thus, if we find that differences between regions are explained by such social variables, we are not seeking to explain them away, as it were. For example, it remains the case that being old in the Borders will not be the same as being old in, say, Glasgow; and being working class in the Highlands is likely to be different from being working class in Edinburgh. In other words, even where we find that attitudinal differences between regions are reducible to the social characteristics of their populations, we are still saying something important about territorial differences per se. We are likely to encounter cultural and political frameworks which operate to make sense of social experiences in different areas, reinforced by the patina of history.

169

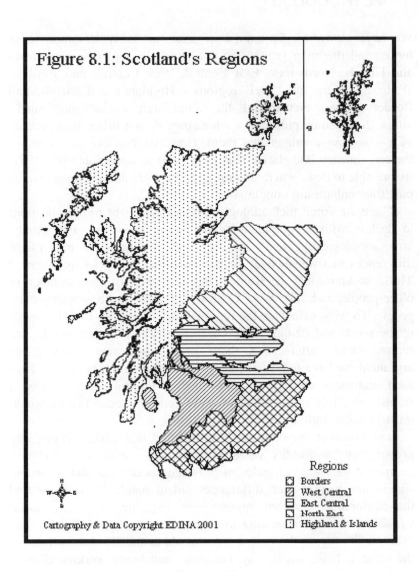

Figure 8.1: Scotland's Regions

Regions
- Borders
- West Central
- East Central
- North East
- Highland & Islands

Cartography & Data Copyright EDINA 2001

This is what we are trying to get at through the kind of analysis given here, rather than attempting to 'explain away' regional differences in terms of social characteristics. There is a further aspect to this. We have chosen to focus primarily on regions rather than on urban-rural differences – measured here by population density – though we do pay attention to these where appropriate. We have chosen to do this in large part because what is meant by urban-rural these days is increasingly open to question, for we do not inhabit a world in which this is a neat and meaningful divide. Thus, many people will live in the 'country' but work, and shop, and entertain themselves in towns and cities. Only quite remote areas of the Highlands and the Borders will be 'genuinely' rural, and, of course, the number of people living in such areas is too small to analyse in much depth, though we endeavour to explore this aspect where it seems to matter.

POLITICS, DEVOLUTION AND IDENTITY

We begin our analysis with an exploration of the more 'political' aspects.

Table 8.2 Party identification

	High-lands	North East	East Central	West Central	Borders	All
	%	%	%	%	%	%
Con	14	25	16	13	19	16
Lab	29	20	40	45	23	36
Lib Dem	16	9	11	3	11	8
SNP	21	25	19	16	25	20
None	12	12	9	11	16	11
Sample size	141	298	473	646	105	1663

Source: Scottish Social Attitudes 2000

In terms of how people choose to identify themselves with political parties, there are important regional differences. Thus, while the central belt regions, west and east, are strongly Labour, identifications in the other regions are much more evenly spread.

NATIONAL IDENTITY

The Borders stands out as quite distinct in terms of national identity: nearly half of its residents say they are exclusively Scottish, but this region also contains the highest proportion of people saying they are :clusively British. While a region with a high proportion of elderly people and those born in England (15 per cent compared with only five per cent in West Central Scotland) should also have a higher proportion choosing a British identity, as we found, the existence of such a strong sense of Scottishness is perhaps surprising. Living in such close proximity to the border with England may well contribute towards this sense of distinctiveness. The average number of years people had lived in their particular area was highest in the Borders (25 years), and lowest in the North East (just over 16 years).

Table 8.3 National identity by region

	High-lands	North East	East Central	West Central	Borders	All
	%	%	%	%	%	%
Scottish, not British	31	33	33	36	45	35
More Scottish than British	26	31	33	37	18	33
Equally Scottish/British	22	22	21	20	22	21
More British than Scottish	6	4	3	2	3	3
British, not Scottish	4	7	4	2	8	4
Sample size	271	489	897	1323	165	3145

Source: Scottish Parliamentary Election Study 1999; and Scottish Social Attitudes 2000

Consistent with what we might expect from the fact that so few people in West Central Scotland are born in England (five per cent, compared with 15 per cent in the Borders) we find this region has the lowest proportion of people choosing to emphasise a British identity over a Scottish one.

We used a statistical model (see the appendix to this book for a detailed description of the technique) to identify which factors are associated with people saying they are Scottish, not British. This model, and most of the others used in the chapter, looked at the following factors: age, sex, class, income and education levels, party identification, Scottish constitutional preference, population density, and finally region, in order to see which have an independent association with our item of interest (in this case Scottish identity). Many of these factors interrelate – such as class and education – and the model can take this into account and identify which has the most significant impact. The most important feature of such models, in this context, is that they can identify whether region per se is a significant factor, once the social characteristics of the regions (such as age and education levels) have been controlled for.

In this first model we find that region, along with education, constitutional preference, and party identification, are the most significant. The region with the lowest likelihood of people saying they are exclusively Scottish is the Highlands and Islands, whereas those living in the Borders were most likely to say they were Scottish. We can conclude, therefore, that there is a 'regional' effect on identity even when the social characteristics of these regions are controlled for.

CONSTITUTIONAL PREFERENCES

What of preferred constitutional option? Table 8.4 shows that no particular region stands out as significantly distinct from the rest in terms of support for independence. Support for devolution (either with or without tax varying powers) is highest in the East Central region and lowest in the Borders, with small but marginally higher levels of support for the 'no devolution' option appearing in the Borders and North East. These regional differences are statistically significant.

SCOTTISH-ENGLISH CONFLICT

And what of tensions between England and Scotland? Do people living close to the border feel this more intensely than maybe those farthest away?

Table 8.4 Constitutional preference by region

	High-lands	North East	East Central	West Central	Borders	All
	%	%	%	%	%	%
Independence	32	26	27	30	31	29
Devolution	55	56	60	57	50	57
No devolution	11	15	10	9	14	11
Sample size	271	489	897	1323	165	3145

Source: Scottish Parliamentary Election Study 1999; and Scottish Social Attitudes 2000

Table 8.5 Scottish-English conflict by region

	High-lands	North East	East Central	West Central	Borders	All
	%	%	%	%	%	%
Very/fairly serious	37	35	38	44	44	40
Not very serious	52	55	55	48	46	51
There is no conflict	10	10	7	6	10	8
Sample size	271	489	897	1323	165	3145

Source: Scottish Parliamentary Election Study 1999; and Scottish Social Attitudes 2000

The difference in attitudes between the Highlands and Borders does not approach statistical significance. However, the difference between the Highlands and West Central Scotland is significant, as is the difference between the Borders and the North East. However the fact that there is also a significant difference between East and West Central Scotland suggest that something other than geography is at work here. East Central Scotland contains lower proportions of working class people, and higher proportions of middle class professionals than West Central Scotland and the Borders, and if we look at the relationship between class and perceptions of English-Scottish conflict we find that working class people are three times as likely to say there is very serious conflict as are the professional middle classes. The role of social rather than regional factors in accounting for differences in attitudes is confirmed by the fact that region does not feature in the statistical model designed to identify the factors associated with the perception that conflict between England and Scotland is very serious.

ATTITUDES TO THE UNION

Does this pattern carry over into attitudes towards the economic benefits of the Union? The Highlands and Borders have identical views when it comes to the belief that England is benefiting most from the Union (47 per cent), and East Central Scotland is the least likely to think this (39 per cent). Around one third in each region think that both countries benefit equally.

When people were asked about government spending, again we find that the views of those in the Highlands and Borders are identical, and by combining these groups we can see more clearly that it is in fact the East Central region which stands out as believing that Scotland gets more than its fair share, and the North East which thinks Scotland gets much less than its fair share.

ATTITUDES TOWARDS GOVERNANCE

We saw that support for devolved administration in Scotland is lowest in the Borders and highest in the East Central Scotland (where it is actually located). Does this mean that perceptions of the Parliament's impact and support for increasing its powers varies regionally?

Table 8.6 Attitudes to Scotland's share of government spending by region

	Highlands & Borders	North East	East Central	West Central	All
	%	%	%	%	%
Much or a little more	8	10	13	9	10
Pretty much its fair share	31	23	28	26	27
Much or little less	57	65	55	59	59
Sample size	246	298	474	646	1663

Source: Scottish Social Attitudes 2000

Table 8.7 shows answers to a question about whether the introduction of the Scottish Parliament has improved the way in which Britain is governed. (The reader should bear in mind that this survey was carried out in 2000, one year after the Parliament was set up.) The Borders stand out as thinking that it has made no difference, and those in the Highlands are twice as likely as those in the Borders to say that it is still too early to say. (This last option was not explicitly presented to respondents, but was recorded if respondents volunteered it, and so many more may have chosen it had it been offered.)

The regional variations in the referendum results noted previously might suggest that the parts of Scotland with the least enthusiasm for the very existence of the Parliament would also have pretty low expectations of its performance. Looking at such expectations in relation to a number of policy areas reveals that the picture is somewhat more complicated. The Highlands and Islands as a region did not vote uniformly when it came to the referendum, and our sample size here is in no way large enough to reflect that diversity. So, when we look at the region as a whole it actually stands out as having the highest expectations of whether the parliament is going to improve the standard of education, give ordinary people in Scotland more say in its governance and give Scotland a stronger voice in the UK. The weak endorsement the Borders gave the parliament in the referendum does seem to be reflected in low expectations of its capacity to improve education – just one third (35 per cent) said that the Parliament is improving education, whereas half (52 per cent) of the respondents from the Highlands and Islands said that this was the case. However the Borders is not particularly distinct on any of our other expectations measures, so it would be wrong to conclude that this region is systematically distinctive in terms of the variables we have been exploring.

Table 8.7 Scottish Parliament and the governance of Britain by region

	High-lands	North East	East Central	West Central	Borders	All
	%	%	%	%	%	%
Improved it a lot/little	34	33	38	33	30	34
Made no difference	39	44	42	44	55	44
Made it little/lot worse	8	13	9	10	5	10
(Too early to tell)	13	8	7	11	6	9
Sample size	141	298	473	646	105	1663

Source: Scottish Social Attitudes 2000

There are no discernible differences between the regions in terms of whether people think the Scottish Parliament or Westminster does or should have most influence over the running of Scotland. Around one in ten think that the Scottish Parliament does have most influence, whereas around seven in ten think it should have most influence.

We asked whether people agreed or disagreed that the Scottish Parliament should be granted more powers. In broad terms there was no real differences between the regions. However, when we look at the strength of opinion, we find quite a stark difference. Almost twice as many people in the Highlands as in the Borders said they agreed strongly that it should have more powers (32 per cent compared to 18 per cent). So while overall support seems similar, people in the Borders are much less emphatic in their views regarding this matter, although it should be pointed out that no such differences, in terms of region or emphasis, occur when it comes to disagreement that the Parliament should have more powers.

There was no regional difference in views about the reduction of the powers of Scottish MPs at Westminster, with around half agreeing that they should no longer be allowed to vote on English matters.

Looking at attitudes towards the current system of governing Britain, we see that the Borders stands out as the most satisfied with the way things are, and that people in the North East are the most likely to want some further change.

Using a model to identify what factors have the greatest influence on whether people think the current system of governing Britain works well or just needs small improvements, we find that Conservative and Labour party identifiers are more likely to think this than, unsurprisingly, supporters of the Scottish National Party. Similarly those whose constitutional preference is independence, rather than devolution, are least likely to take this view. Men, and people with high household incomes, were also more likely to be satisfied with the current system of governing Britain. In addition to these factors, however, region was also found to be significant. Confirming the findings in Table 8.8, people in the Highlands and Islands have the most favourable view of the system of governing Britain, whereas those in the North East and West Central Scotland are least satisfied.

EUROPE

What of attitudes to Europe, the other key political dimension? The Highlands and Islands region is the most positive when it comes to the question of whether the EU has been good or bad for Scotland, although this is perhaps because European funds have been invested in the Highlands as a result of its Objective 1 status (which is now being phased out). People in the Borders, on the other hand, are less sure of the benefits of being part of the EU.

Table 8.8 Attitudes to the way Britain is governed, by region

	High-lands	North East	East Central	West Central	Borders	All
	%	%	%	%	%	%
Works extremely well/small improvement needed	43	29	32	30	39	32
Could be improved quite a bit	44	55	51	50	43	50
Needs a great deal of improvement	11	15	16	18	17	16
Sample size	141	298	473	646	105	1663

Source: Scottish Social Attitudes 2000

Table 8.9 The EU and Scotland, by region

	Highlands	North East	East Central	West Central	Borders	All
	%	%	%	%	%	%
Good for Scotland	50	33	42	36	26	38
Bad for Scotland	22	25	20	20	25	21
Neither or both	16	30	24	27	34	26
Don't know	12	12	14	16	16	14
Sample size	271	489	897	1323	165	3145

Source: Scottish Parliamentary Election Study 1999; and Scottish Social Attitudes 2000

The Highlands' ringing endorsement of the EU's impact does not, however, lead to distinctly positive feelings about the scope of the EU or about the Euro. The view that Britain should leave the EU altogether is held by around one in ten people across the regions. The strongest backing for the EU comes, in fact, from East Central Scotland where just over one quarter (27 per cent) support the EU either having more powers, or moving towards a single European state.

Table 8.10 Britain and the EU, by region

Britain should...	High- lands	North East	East Central	West Central	Borders	All
	%	%	%	%	%	%
Leave the EU	13	13	9	10	11	11
Stay, but reduce EU powers	41	44	36	33	34	36
Leave things as they are	22	19	20	22	29	21
Stay, but increase EU powers	11	9	17	14	13	14
Work towards a single European government	8	8	9	9	5	9
Sample size	271	489	897	1323	165	3145

Source: Scottish Parliamentary Election Study 1999; and Scottish Social Attitudes 2000

This trend is also picked up in support for the Euro, where again people in East Central Scotland are most in favour.

Table 8.11 Britain and the Euro, by region

Britain should…	High-lands	North East	East Central	West Central	Borders	All
	%	%	%	%	%	%
Join the Euro	35	31	39	34	31	35
Not join the Euro	54	58	50	53	57	53
Don't know	11	11	11	13	12	12
Sample size	271	489	897	1323	165	3145

Source: Scottish Parliamentary Election Study 1999; and Scottish Social Attitudes 2000

TRANSPORT

As a relatively sparsely populated country, as well as one with a preponderance of people living in the Central Belt, Scotland might be expected to generate considerable differences in attitudes to transport.

Starting with a very general – but highly pertinent – question, we asked people to say whether they agreed or disagreed with the following statement:

For the sake of the environment, car users should pay higher taxes.

Just one in ten people agreed. Despite their similar profiles in terms of urban-rural density and perhaps similar problems with regard to roads and access to a full public transport system, people in the Highlands were twice as likely to agree with this statement as people in the Borders. People in East Central Scotland – which of course includes Edinburgh, the city which has arguably done the most to promote alternatives to car use – had much lower proportions of people disagreeing than for example the North East and the Borders.

Table 8.12 Taxing car users, by region

Car users should pay higher taxes	High-lands	North East	East Central	West Central	Borders	All
	%	%	%	%	%	%
Agree	15	9	11	10	6	10
Disagree	73	80	68	73	84	74
Sample size	117	272	453	561	103	1506

Source: Scottish Social Attitudes 2000

We also asked a number of questions with particular relevance in a regional context (Table 8.13). Firstly, people were asked what they thought about car use in towns and cities, and then in rural areas. The perception clearly is that cars are not needed in urban areas to the extent that they are in rural areas. And, whereas those in the Highlands appear to feel quite strongly that people in towns and cities use cars unnecessarily, all regions have pretty similar views about the necessity of cars in rural areas. Interestingly, but perhaps not surprisingly, there are quite stark variations between the regions when it comes to the strength of disagreement with the view that people in rural areas use their cars unnecessarily. Half of those in the Highlands took the strongest position and said they disagreed strongly, compared with around one third in the Borders and North East and around just one quarter in the East and West Central regions.

It is also worth noting that there is clearly something distinct about opinions on this matter in the Highlands, compared with other regions of Scotland, which cannot be explained simply by urban-rural differences. When we restricted our analysis to just those people in the Borders and Highlands who live in the most rural areas as measured by population density (which still accounts for around 80 per cent of the population of these regions) those in the Highlands are still more likely to disagree strongly that people in rural areas do not need cars than people in the Borders.

Table 8.13 Attitudes to car use in rural and urban areas, by region

% who disagree that you...	High-lands	North East	East Central	West Central	Borders	All
...don't need cars in cities	27	47	46	49	46	46
...don't need cars in rural areas	77	73	70	77	72	74
Sample size	117	272	453	561	103	1506

Source: Scottish Social Attitudes 2000

Despite this strong support for the view that cars are an essential part of life in the Highlands, support for more motorway building is lowest in this region. Under half (40 per cent) of those in the Highlands agreed that the government should build more motorways, compared with 60 per cent in the Borders (where road improvements are a major political issue), 55 per cent in the North East and in West Central Scotland, and 45 per cent in East Central Scotland.

We also asked whether government should support loss-making public transport services in urban and rural areas. We have already seen that the use of cars in rural areas was more acceptable than in urban areas, and for these items this pattern is in essence mirrored as more people (31 per cent) strongly agree that government should support loss-making transport services in rural areas than do so for urban areas, where 20 per cent strongly agree. There are no particularly notable differences across the regions when it comes to subsidising public transport in the way there was for the questions about the necessity, or otherwise, of car use.

POLITICAL TRUST, SOCIAL CAPITAL AND COMMUNITY INVOLVEMENT

POLITICAL TRUST AND EFFICACY

While trust in government per se does not vary dramatically across Scotland, we do find that people in the Highlands are more trusting than those in West Central Scotland. This is also reflected in a series of questions designed to measure the extent to which people think the political system is responsive to their demands, and whether they are personally capable of influencing it (concepts often referred to as personal and system efficacy respectively). On the whole, people in the Highlands have the highest levels of efficacy.

People in the Borders are the most likely to think that MPs lose touch with people once they are elected, and the belief that MPs don't care what people think is strongest in the West Central region and the Borders, whereas just half of those in the Highlands think this is the case. The belief that 'it doesn't matter which party is in power, things go on much the same' is shared equally across the regions.

Table 8.14 Political efficacy by region

% who agree that	High-lands	North East	East Central	West Central	Borders	All
Parties are only interested in votes	60	72	72	76	76	73
It doesn't matter who's in power, things go on much the same	73	76	75	76	80	75
MPs don't care what people like me think	53	61	61	65	66	62
MPs soon lose touch with people	65	71	72	73	78	72
Sample size	141	298	473	646	105	1663

Source: Scottish Social Attitudes 2000

To examine these concepts of system and personal efficacy further we combined the responses to the four questions shown in Table 8.14 to produce a single measure of people's level of efficacy. We then used a statistical model designed to identify the factors associated with having low levels of efficacy. Having no educational qualifications, a low income, and identifying with the SNP were all associated with having low efficacy. Supporting what we found in Table 8.14, region also emerges as having an independent association with levels of efficacy. People in the North East and West Central Scotland were most likely to have low levels of efficacy, and those in the Highlands and Islands were most likely to have the highest levels. This relationship between region, most notably the Highlands and Islands, and efficacy echoes our earlier discussion of perceptions of the current system of governing Britain where we also found this region to be the least dissatisfied with the status quo.

PUBLIC SPENDING AND SOCIAL POLICY

In terms of spending priorities, the regions are united in their desire for extra health spending as a first priority (six in ten say this), and over 40 per cent give education as their second priority. However, looking at some of the less commonly opted-for spending areas highlights some interesting differences. Although small, the proportion of people in the Borders saying help for industry was their first priority for extra spending was six per cent compared with just one per cent in East and West Central Scotland.

When asked about taxation and spending, people in the Borders are the least likely to want higher taxes and increased spending (48 per cent), whereas people in West Central Scotland are most likely to want this (57 per cent).

Regional patterns of unemployment could feasibly result in regional differences in attitudes towards unemployment benefits. And this is in fact the case, with nearly half (45 per cent) of those in West Central Scotland saying that unemployment benefit was too low, whereas one third thought this in the Borders (32 per cent) and the North East (31 per cent). Conversely, people living in the Borders and the Highlands were the most likely to say that unemployment benefit is too high and that it discourages people from finding work. However, such apparently strong regional differences appear to be explained in large part by the strongly significant relationship between age and attitudes to unemployment benefit, rather than region per se.

185

Perceptions of income inequality were uniform across the regions, around 85 per cent thinking that the gap between those with high and low incomes is too large. People in the North East are the most likely to say they have a high income, and least likely to say they have a low income. Those in the Borders and West Central Scotland were most likely to say they had a low income (49 and 52 per cent respectively).

In part reflecting this, people in the North East and West Central Scotland were most likely to say they were living comfortably on their present income with 40 per cent saying this, compared with just 28 per cent in the Borders.

PARTICIPATION AND COMMUNITY ACTIVITIES

Issues of access are also linked to issues of participation, and in this section we explore how involved people are in social activities, and how willing they are to take part in protest.

When asked about hypothetical actions that they might take against an unjust law, people in the Borders clearly stand out: 16 per cent said that they would take no action, compared with levels of between three and six per cent for the other regions. Those aged over 60 are the least likely to say they would take any actions which could lead us to conclude that the age profile of the Borders accounts for this notably high level saying they would take no action. However, using a statistical model of the kind we have described already, we found that people in the Borders stand out as being significantly more likely to say they'd take no action even when age has been taken into account. People with no qualifications, those who did not know or would not disclose their household income and people with no party identification were also more likely to say this.

However, when asked whether they had actually taken any of these actions themselves, the pattern is less stark. Around four in ten in each region said they had not engaged in any activities. People in East Central Scotland are the most active, with 13 per cent saying that they had engaged in a minimum of five protest activities, whereas half as many (six per cent) in the Borders had done so.

Table 8.15 Protest action, by region

% who...	High- lands	North East	East Central	West Central	Borders	All
Would take no action	3	6	5	5	16	5
Have taken no action	39	37	40	42	43	40
Have taken 5+ actions	10	7	13	7	6	9
Sample size	141	298	473	646	105	1663

Source: Scottish Social Attitudes 2000

People living in the Highlands and Islands are more likely to be involved in sports and cultural organisations (four in ten), whereas the figure for the rest of the regions is around one quarter. When we used a statistical model to examine this, we found that region per se seems to be a less significant predictor of such social activity than population density, for people in sparsely populated parts of Scotland are the most likely to be members of such groups, and this would seem to explain why the Highlands and Islands appear to have higher participation rates. The fact that having a high income and high levels of education were also important determinants of whether people join such organisations helps account for the fact that although the population densities of the two regions are very similar, the Borders (which has the highest proportion of people with no qualifications, and generally lower incomes than the rest of Scotland) does not stand out as a region with many people joining sports and cultural groups. There are, however, no significant differences between the regions when it comes to membership of community organisations.

Table 8.16 Organisational membership, by region

% who are	High-lands	North East	East Central	West Central	Borders	All
Members of sports or cultural group	39	26	28	26	25	37
Members of 1+ local community organisation	20	26	21	21	18	22
Sample size	141	298	473	646	105	1663

Source: Scottish Social Attitudes 2000

Table 8.17 Social trust, by region

% who would be very comfortable asking a neighbour to…	High-lands	North East	East Central	West Central	Borders	All
…collect a prescription	80	59	53	56	64	58
…borrow a sink plunger	80	61	60	60	68	62
…borrow £5 for milkman	36	25	19	19	33	22
% who would feel very comfortable asking a passer by for directions if lost	56	44	47	44	65	47
Sample size	141	298	473	646	105	1663

Source: Scottish Social Attitudes 2000

SOCIAL TRUST AND NEIGHBOURLINESS

On a range of measures looking at social trust, we can see that the Highlands tends to stand out as somewhere with high levels of trust in others and where people feel comfortable in asking others for help in times of need. However, when asked about relying on strangers, as opposed to neighbours, people from the Borders and the Highlands are most likely to feel happy about approaching strangers for directions when lost in an unfamiliar place.

Looking at measures of social isolation reveals that – perhaps surprisingly – people in the Borders are the most likely to say that they would turn to no-one if they needed to talk to someone about feeling down or depressed, or if they were thinking of moving to another part of the country. (The question asked people to choose someone other than their partner as a possible person to talk to).

Table 8.18 Social support, by region

% who would turn to no-one...	High-lands	North East	East Central	West Central	Borders	All
...if they were feeling down or depressed	5	7	6	8	13	7
...if they were thinking of moving to another part of the country	6	8	7	8	16	8
Sample size	117	272	453	561	103	1506

Source: Scottish Social Attitudes 2000

THE MORAL MAP

The conventional view that the more rural parts of Scotland such as the Borders and Highlands and Islands are more socially and morally conservative appears to be borne out by findings on a range of attitudes to such issues. Thus, with regard to attitudes to homosexuality, half of those living in the Highlands and Borders (compared with only a third of people in East Central Scotland) said that it was always wrong. One in three in East Central Scotland also said it was not at all wrong, compared with one in six in the Borders.

We asked about abortion under two different circumstances: if there is a serious defect in the baby, or if the family is too poor to keep the baby. Perhaps not surprisingly, for both scenarios those in West Central Scotland stand out as being most opposed to abortion.

Table 8.19 Attitudes to abortion, by region

% who say it is always or almost always wrong to have an abortion	High- lands	North East	East Central	West Central	Borders	All
… if there is a serious defect in the baby	9	14	15	20	11	16
…if the family cannot afford to keep the baby	34	36	34	43	36	38
Sample size	117	272	453	561	103	1506

Source: Scottish Social Attitudes 2000

The view that people who want children should marry beforehand is held by over one quarter (27 per cent) of those in the Highlands but just 16 per cent of those in the Borders. However, this is an artefact of the strength of opinion, as 50 per cent across the board agree or agree strongly. In fact there is little real difference in views about marriage and cohabitation, which is to an extent to be expected, given the fact that differences between the regions in terms of marital status do not differ.

Table 8.20 Attitudes to marriage and cohabitation, by region

% who agree strongly that	High-lands	North East	East Central	West Central	Borders	All
People who want children should marry first	27	20	18	23	16	21
Marriage is the best kind of relationship	22	14	15	14	13	15
Married couples are better parents	15	7	8	9	7	8
It is alright to live together without marrying	20	14	19	16	13	17
It is a good idea to live together before marriage	20	18	17	15	18	17
Sample size	117	272	453	561	103	1506

Source: Scottish Social Attitudes 2000

We also find that half of people in the Borders said that sex before marriage is not at all wrong, whereas this figure is around six in ten everywhere else. Underage sex is disapproved of generally, with around seven in ten in all regions saying it is always wrong, as is extra-marital sex.

People living in East Central Scotland take the most liberal view of drugs, in this instance the legalisation of cannabis.

Table 8.21 Attitudes to the legalisation of cannabis, by region

	High- lands	North East	East Central	West Central	Borders	All
	%	%	%	%	%	%
Be legal, or available in licensed shops only	46	49	53	46	44	48
Remain illegal	52	50	47	52	56	50
Sample size	141	298	473	646	105	1663

Source: Scottish Social Attitudes 2000

So, in general, what we seem to have is a Scotland made up of differing views on a variety of moral issues. However there is no one clear picture – the Highlands and the Borders have very distinct views about homosexuality, the Borders are less permissive when it comes to pre-marital sex, people in East Central Scotland are the most liberal about cannabis, and religious differences only seem to play a part in the story when it comes to abortion, where the impact of the high proportion of Catholics in West Central Scotland is quite apparent.

These seemingly 'regional' differences in moral matters do, however, seem to have more to do with the social characteristics of the populations of regions than with regional identity itself. Thus, attitudes to abortion seem to have much more to do with religion, gender, and levels of education and income than region. Similarly, age, education and religion are much stronger predictors of attitudes to homosexuality than region. Region as such does not emerge as significant, although population density is, suggesting that people living in urban areas, especially the cities, are more liberal on these matters.

CONCLUSIONS

Let us return to the questions we raised at the outset. Is Scotland a regionally diverse nation? The answer is yes, for there are important and ongoing differences in social, political and moral attitudes. Is it, then, a divergent nation, in which regional differences are becoming stronger, perhaps making it a more difficult country to govern? Strictly speaking our data do not allow us to make a definitive answer because the time-series is as yet limited to two years (1999 and 2000). Nevertheless, we would be hard pushed to conclude that the regional differences are becoming greater. With regard to political issues, notably to the Scottish Parliament and to trust in political institutions more generally, the similarities between Scotland's regions are much greater than the differences. We do not find, for example, that the more rural regions are the most dissatisfied with the new parliament. The Highlands and Islands have relatively high expectations of its performance whereas the Borders are notably lukewarm. Nevertheless, we might expect regional differences to play an important part in Scotland's politics if only because the electoral system, notably the 'list' voting system, encourages politicians to pay attention to local and regional issues. Even at a Westminster level, where first-past-the-post operates, we find significant regional variations: in the 2001 UK General Election multi-party competition was important, especially in the Highlands and Islands, North East Scotland, and the Borders.

Table 8.22 Vote by region at British General Election 2001

% share of vote	Highlands	North-East	East Central	West Central	Borders
Con	14.2	18.6	16.6	12.3	25.6
Lab	27.5	32.4	44.1	53.9	29.5
Lib-Dem	33.3	19.0	17.6	10.2	26.1
SNP	21.4	27.0	18.1	18.5	16.5
SSP	2.7	2.0	2.6	4.3	1.7
Others	1.0	1.0	1.0	1.0	0.6

Source: General Election results, June 2001

What our survey of Scottish social attitudes shows quite clearly is that rural regions of Scotland, such as the Highlands and Islands and the Borders, are quite unlike each other. While we might have expected that their low population densities (around 80 per cent of the population in each case live in sparsely populated areas) would produce similarities, it is clear that in attitudinal terms they differ quite noticeably.

In both the Highlands and Islands and the Borders, issues of transport have high salience, and further work is needed here. In the Borders in particular, improving transport links – rail and road – has acquired considerable public and political salience as a means of economic regeneration. The Borders has an ageing population not simply because people come to retire there, from England as well as Scotland, but because it has difficulty in retaining its young people for post-school education and employment. Research has shown that young people in the Borders feel they must leave if they want to get on in life (Jamieson 2000).

The Highlands and Islands, on the other hand, is noticeably different in its social and political attitudes. It has the highest level of political trust in governments and politicians of any of Scotland's regions, as well as the highest levels of social trust and community involvement. This latter aspect does seem to be, however, a feature of sparsely populated areas in Scotland, suggesting that viewing rural areas as socially isolating is somewhat wide of the mark.

Neither can we conclude that rural Scotland is a seedbed of moral and social conservatism, for while rural regions, especially the Borders, do at first glance appear to be so, further analysis indicates that this is much more a feature of their social composition (notably age structure) than anything pertaining to the region per se. Nevertheless, people living in urban areas, mainly the large cities, do tend to be more socially and morally liberal in their attitudes.

Nevertheless, many of the differences identified between the regions are in fact explained by their demographic make-up, be it their age, class or educational profile. If significant efforts are made to alter these profiles, such as widening access to higher education, or through economic regeneration and improved transport infrastructures, then it is within Scotland's capacity to reduce regional inequalities if it so desires. Where region is an independent factor then clearly some more intangible force – such as culture or history – is at play, and here we must 'wait and see' what the future holds. Regionalism in Scotland is also susceptible to political changes. Thus, we have found that regional differences are the most significant in the political/efficacy sphere, and any move away to replace the regional 'list' system for the second vote with an all-Scottish one would be most likely to damage levels of trust and efficacy in the very region – Highlands and Islands – where they seem to be holding up against the national trend.

In conclusion, then, we find some important and interesting regional variations in Scotland in terms of the range of social and political attitudes we have been studying in the 1999 and 2000 surveys. Some of these variations, to be sure, relate to urban-rural differences, and others to the social composition of the regions themselves, but we can identify differences that do seem to pertain to region per se. Much more needs to be done to explore this important dimension of Scottish life in surveys to come, but this analysis does enough to suggest that Scotland is indeed a regionally diverse country, if not quite as 'indefinable' as Robert Louis Stevenson imagined.

REFERENCES

Jamieson, L. (2000), 'Migration, place and class: youth in a rural area', *The Sociological Review*, 48, pp. 203-33.

Nairn, T. (1997), *Faces of Nationalism: Janus Revisited*, London: Verso.

Pattie, C., Denver, D., Mitchell, J., and Bochel, H. (1998), 'The 1997 Scottish Referendum: an analysis of the results', *Scottish Affairs*, 22, pp. 1-15.

Smout, T. C. (1994), 'Perspectives on the Scottish identity', *Scottish Affairs*, no. 6, pp. 101-13.

Stevenson, R. L. (1895), *The Silverado Squatters*, London: Chatto and Windus.

9

GOVERNING FROM THE CENTRE: IDEOLOGY AND PUBLIC POLICY

LINDSAY PATERSON

INTRODUCTION

New Labour has made a virtue of governing from the centre. Tony Blair rarely talks of the simple 'left' approvingly, reserving his approbation for the 'centre left'. He has repeatedly argued that the centre left in Britain suffered a debilitating split when the Labour Party was formed in the early part of the twentieth century: except in the decade following 1945, anti-Tory votes were thus divided between the Labour Party and the Liberals or their successors. He put this point unambiguously in a speech during the 2001 UK general election campaign, when he said that the political tradition to which he was heir was not mainly the twentieth-century tradition of the Labour Party on its own, but what he called 'the moderate Labour movement and Liberal Party tradition of the nineteenth century' (Blair 2001).

The particular trauma for New Labour politicians in this respect was the electoral defeat of 1983, when (in Britain as a whole) the Labour Party and the alliance between the Liberals and the Social Democratic Party received almost the same share of the vote, allowing Margaret Thatcher to achieve her most emphatic victory. The conventional wisdom in the party was that this defeat was because of the socialist manifesto which Labour adopted for the election. The whole process of so-called modernisation which then followed – under Neil Kinnock, John Smith and Blair – was a process of gradually shifting the party towards the centre (as well as renovating its organisational capacity and its constitution).

That historic split, reaching its nadir in 1983, was not the only source of pressure towards the centre. Another was the perception that Thatcher had caused great damage to social cohesion because she had governed firmly from a definitely off-centre position on the political spectrum. Her most radical initiatives – such as selling off nationalised industries, giving priority to reducing inflation over reducing unemployment, and preferring tax cuts to improving public services – were taken against the views of majorities in the population (Heath et al 2001: 31-57). A common analysis in the Labour Party was then that their 1983 manifesto had reacted in the wrong way. It had lurched to an opposite extreme from Thatcher, whereas what was needed was to re-assert the virtues of compromise and consensus. That view was particularly prominent in Scotland, and became one of the most influential sources of the idea that a Scottish Parliament should work by consultation rather than imposition.

This whole centrist philosophy, of course, has now been described as a 'third way', one interpretation of which is as a middle point between left and right, although – still aware of the rather unattractive aura which compromise acquired in the 1970s – the ideologues of the third way tend to prefer to say that it transcends left and right, rather than stands in the middle between them (Giddens 1994, 1998). Blair's own view is that 'the Third Way is not an attempt to split the difference between Right and Left. It is about traditional values in a changing world', by which he meant the old liberal tradition again: 'it draws vitality from uniting the two great streams of left-of-centre thought – democratic socialism and liberalism' (Blair 1998: 1).

Grand historical aspirations of this sort would presumably, however, be of little appeal to the party if the notion of a renovated centre did not also appeal to that part of the electorate which actually occupies the centre ground. That, after all, was the first reason why Blair deplored the left-of-centre divisions, and why the party reacted so thoroughly to their 1983 experience. It was not on philosophical grounds that Kinnock, Smith and Blair invented New Labour: it was to win elections. So the concept of the 'centre-left' is not mainly a matter of party or government ideology on its own: it must also to a large extent be whether and how party thinking corresponds to the thinking of that broad block of electors who are not at either end of the left-right spectrum.

So what does the centre look like? Is Labour truly governing according to principles that would be acceptable in that centre? How would that differ from views on the left, where the party has historically situated itself? How might the views of the centre be changing? Does government help to shape the views of the centre, as Thatcher seems to have done, for example on privatisation, although not on taxes and spending (Heath et al 2001: 31-57)?

And might the answers to these questions be different in Scotland and England? Labour faces a more vigorous left-wing opposition in Scotland – in the shape of a somewhat more social democratic Scottish National Party and the firmly left-wing Scottish Socialist Party. The 1983 election was not the disaster for the Scottish Labour Party that it was for the party in England: Labour won 35 per cent of the vote, more than ten points ahead of the Alliance, and seven points ahead of the Conservatives. The Scottish Labour Party prided itself in believing that this was partly because it had never indulged in the left-wing excesses which allegedly had engulfed the party in the south. Now that Labour leads the government in the Scottish Parliament, it appears to be pursuing more traditionally left-wing policies on some matters than the government in London. The new arrangements for student finance aim to redistribute resources from relatively wealthy graduates in the form of bursaries for poor students. The proposed arrangements for state payment of the care costs of old people are a form of universal benefit that New Labour is supposed to believe to be inefficient in comparison with means-tested payments.

This chapter examines the views and characteristics of three broad ideological groups in Scotland and England – the left, the centre and the right. It looks at views on selected policy topics, some within the competence of the Scottish Parliament and some mostly reserved to the UK Parliament, at party allegiance, at views on how the powers of the Scottish Parliament should develop, and at some of the sociological characteristics of the ideological groups. Where possible, the evolution of views in the groups between 1999 and 2000 is traced. Two main questions guide the analysis and discussion. Is the Scottish centre notably different from that in England? And is government policy in Scotland closer or less close to the Scottish centre than government policy in England is to the English centre?

Two further clarifications of what we are doing here are important. The attention is to ideological positions, not to individuals. The premises on which the chapter is based are that there is a meaningful ideological debate on the left-right dimension, that there are recognisable positions within that debate that can be approximately labelled as 'left', 'right' and 'centre', and that studying the views and characteristics of these three groups is interesting. For our purposes here, it does not matter whether individuals are wholly consistent in the ways in which they translate ideological commitment into views about specific policy. Nor does it matter if, over time, individuals move between ideological groups. All we are interested in is the ideological groups as a whole, regardless of the possible idiosyncrasies of the individuals who happen to make up the groups at any particular time.

The other clarification concerns why we concentrate on the left-right dimension of ideology. The main reason is because that is how the issue tends to be put by New Labour politicians – for example, by Tony Blair, as we have seen. Political scientists have also recently investigated other dimensions of ideology, notably that between libertarianism and authoritarianism (Heath et al 1994). A fuller analysis would look at this too, but the question of the significance of left-right ideology is interesting regardless of the significance of other ways of categorising beliefs.

DEFINING THE CENTRE

Ideology is not amenable to being measured directly by survey research. What we can do, however, is to construct a scale of political values from a group of questions relating to issues that are salient in debates between left and right. This approach is very common in the study of popular ideology (Heath et al 1994). For the British and Scottish Social Attitudes Surveys in 2000, we use the five questions shown in Table 9.1, where the distribution of responses in Scotland and England is also shown. The scale is constructed by assigning the value 1 to the most left-wing position ('agree strongly'), and so on through to 5 for the most right-wing position ('disagree strongly'), and then adding up the resulting values for each individual in the sample. These totals are divided by 5 (the number of questions) to give a range from 1 to 5. Thus scale values near 1 are left wing, and values near 5 are right wing.

Table 9.1 Components of left-right scale, Scotland and England, 2000

row percentages	agree strongly	agree	neither agree nor disagree	disagree	disagree strongly
redistribution					
Scotland	14	36	24	22	2
England	9	29	24	31	6
big business benefits owners					
Scotland	13	48	24	11	1
England	12	43	26	16	2
working people do not get fair share					
Scotland	16	55	18	8	1
England	13	48	24	12	1
one law for rich and one for poor					
Scotland	24	43	17	13	1
England	20	43	18	16	2
management tries to get better of employees					
Scotland	19	43	20	15	1
England	15	45	22	15	1

Don't know and not answered included in base.

Percentages are weighted; for sample sizes, see Table 9.2.

source: Scottish Social Attitudes Survey 2000 and British Social Attitudes Survey 2000.

The 'left', 'centre' and 'right' are then defined as those people with scale values that are low, medium and high. By doing this separately for Scotland and England, we allow for the possibility that the Scottish 'centre' might be different from the English one. Exactly where the boundaries should be placed between these ideological groups is a matter of somewhat arbitrary judgement. The over-riding concern here was to get roughly the same proportion of the Scottish and English respondents in corresponding groups, subject to the left and right groups each making up around 20-25 per cent of the population, and hence to the centre group constituting around 50-60 per cent. Making three groups about equal in size would have been feasible, but did not correspond to the political philosophy which gave rise to this investigation. The assumption in the New Labour rhetoric of governing from the centre is that the centre is large. A group consisting of one third of the population would not be the basis on which a stable centrist government could be built and maintained. Nevertheless, having said this, the broad patterns we comment on in the chapter did not depend strongly on precisely where the boundaries of the groups were placed.

The closest that could be managed to these principles of definition is that shown in Table 9.2. In Scotland, 18 per cent are on the left, 59 per cent in the centre and 23 per cent on the right. In England, the figures are quite close to these: 19 per cent, 60 per cent and 21 per cent. Getting left and right groups closer to a quarter each was not feasible here, because of the way the values on the scale were clustered. Table 9.2 also shows the range of values on the scale in each of the three groups in each country. It can be seen that the Scottish centre is indeed somewhat to the left of the English centre, although not by much (as could also be deduced from the distribution of the individual items in Table 9.1).

Exactly the same was done for England in 1999, from the 1999 British Social Attitudes Survey. The same survey items could be used as are shown in Table 9.1, and indeed identical ranges of scale values produced very similarly sized ideological groups as in 2000: the proportions in 1999 were 17 per cent, 61 per cent and 22 per cent. This stability between the years tends to add validity to the claim that the scale is measuring underlying political beliefs, rather than ephemeral changes in response to political events.

Unfortunately, the identical approach could not be used for Scotland in 1999, where the five items used to make up the 2000 scale were not asked in the Scottish Social Attitudes Survey. A different set of items was, however, included in that survey, allowing an analogous scale to be constructed (Paterson et al 2001: 178): questions about inequalities of wealth and of power, about the roles of trades unions and of private enterprise, about nationalisation, and about government's responsibility for creating full employment.

These were constructed into a scale as in 2000, and the scale was then used to form three ideological groups in Scotland in 1999. The proportions in them were chosen to be as close as possible to those in Table 9.2: 16 per cent on the left, 65 per cent in the centre, and 18 per cent on the right. If it is correct to assume that the scale reflects ideology on a left-right dimension, then it should be possible to compare ideological groups in 1999 and 2000 even though they were formed using different individual items.

Table 9.2 Ideological groups on left-right scale, Scotland and England, 2000

	left	centre	right	all
Scotland				
range on scale	1.0-1.75	2.0-2.8	3.0-5.0	
size (per cent)	18	59	23	
sample size	283	870	315	1468
England				
range on scale	1.0-1.8	2.0-3.0	3.2-5.0	
size (per cent)	19	60	21	
sample size	486	1501	499	2486

Percentages are weighted; sample sizes are unweighted.

Don't know and not answered included in base (195 cases in Scotland and 401 in England).

Source: Scottish Social Attitudes Survey 2000; British Social Attitudes Survey 2000.

WHAT POLICIES DOES THE CENTRE SUPPORT? (I) DEVOLVED MATTERS

We look at eight policy areas, four mainly devolved to the Scottish Parliament, and four mainly reserved to Westminster. The devolved matters are ones in which there has been a great deal of political debate since the first election to the Parliament in 1999.

The first is attitudes to tuition fees in higher education, where we have questions on the principle in both Scotland and England in both 1999 and 2000. In Scotland in 2000, we have a further question on the new student endowment scheme that is replacing tuition fees paid at the beginning of a student's course: in future, about a half of graduates will be liable to pay into the endowment fund, in a manner that resembles a graduate tax (exemption being given to certain categories of student, such as those who take a higher education diploma rather than a degree, and those who are registered as disabled). In 2000, we also have a question on what should be done with the proceeds of the endowment.

The second devolved matter is homosexuality. We do not have specific questions relating to the controversies over the repeal of Section 2a (Section 28 in the rest of Britain) – the legislation that prevented local authorities (and hence public sector schools) from 'promoting' homosexual relationships as an acceptable basis of family life – but we do have a general question on attitudes to homosexuality. We do not have the question in a form that may be compared between 1999 and 2000, and so we look only at views in 2000 here.

The third devolved matter is also less specific: it simply asks whether government has responsibility for maintaining the living standards of old people. The 2000 survey did not ask about care for the elderly – the precise matter that became controversial later in the year – but this general question might tap general attitudes towards government involvement. We have this question only for 2000, in both Scotland and England.

The fourth devolved matter is on the role of teachers in the education system. Behind the recent new settlement for teachers' pay and conditions in Scotland is apparently a changed view by the Scottish government on the responsibilities which teachers should have. The education minister, Jack McConnell, claimed that he wanted to leave educational professionals to run the education system, and to stop interfering from the centre. The SNP spokesperson on education, Michael Russell, took a similar view, and so this can now be said to be the emerging attitude to teachers among the new Scottish political class. So does it correspond with opinion more generally in Scotland – are people in general favourable to the idea that teachers (not politicians) should be the main influence on the daily management of schools? This question was asked only in Scotland, and only in 2000.

Attitudes to up-front tuition fees are shown in Table 9.3. The most striking first point is that all ideological groups in both countries support a system of means-tested fees. So it is the government in England that is most in touch with opinion, not the Scottish government, which has abolished such fees. It is true that rather larger minorities of people in Scotland than in England support that abolition, but that minority is in fact larger on the right than in the centre. On this matter, the Scottish Labour-led government could not be said to be at the centre. What's more, opinion in the centre and on the left in Scotland actually moved away from the Scottish government's position between 1999 and 2000. In 1999, opposition to all fees was at 52 per cent on the left, and 44 per cent in the centre; it dropped by fifteen and eight points respectively. Only on the right was there a slight movement towards the Scottish government's position, from 43 per cent to 45 per cent. In England, where the government's position is that some students should pay fees, there were drops in opposition to fees in all ideological groups (down four points on the left, ten in the centre, and eight on the right), and so there was a clear movement in the government's direction.

Table 9.3 Attitude to up-front tuition fees, among ideological groups on left-right scale, Scotland and England, 2000

column percentages	Scotland				England			
	left	centre	right	all	left	centre	right	all
All students pay	5	5	4	5	7	7	7	8
Some students pay, depending on their circumstances	57	58	52	56	57	66	59	61
No students pay	37	36	45	38	36	26	34	30

Don't know and not answered included in base.

Percentages are weighted; for sample sizes, see Table 9.2.

source: Scottish Social Attitudes Survey 2000 and British Social Attitudes Survey 2000.

It is true that, in Scotland in 2000, clear majorities support the government's new position that some students should pay the endowment contribution (56 per cent on the left, 53 per cent in the centre, and 46 per cent – the largest group – on the right). But it appears that – unlike the government – popular opinion wants means-tested fees both to be paid in advance and also to be paid as an endowment after graduation. Across the population as a whole, of those who favour the endowment contributions, 76 per cent also favour means-tested up-front fees. Of those opposed to up-front fees, 60 per cent are also opposed to the endowment contribution. The Scottish government's position of ending upfront fees and introducing endowment contributions to be paid by some students is supported by only 11 per cent of the total population, a proportion that does not vary with ideological position.

There is strong support in Scotland for hypothecation of the endowment: in all ideological groups, some 85 per cent believe that the money should be spent on some aspect of higher education, only around 4-5 per cent believing it should be spent on other public services, and only 7-9 per cent believing that it should be used to reduce taxes. Nevertheless, even this is not a straightforward endorsement of the Scottish government's position. Their policy is to use the endowment contributions to fund bursaries for poor students. But spending this money on students is supported by only 38 per cent of left-wing people, 35 per cent of people in the centre, and 22 per cent of people on the right. The balance want the money spent on general university matters: 45 per cent on the left, 50 per cent in the centre, and 63 per cent on the right.

On homosexuality, popular views are polarised, as Table 9.4 shows (and as Chapter 5 discusses more fully). Large minorities in both England and Scotland believe that homosexuality is always wrong, and almost equally large minorities believe it is not wrong at all. Nevertheless, within this, there are interesting ideological differences. If we take the Scottish and English government position to be that people should be free to practice whatever kind of sex they want, then only views towards the bottom end of the table are consistent with government policy. It then appears that the Scottish government view has least support in the centre, although the differences are not large – 37 per cent in the bottom two categories in the centre, compared to 39 per cent on the left and 43 per cent on the right. In England, by contrast, the government position is most popular in the centre (although only just) – 43 per cent, compared to 39 per cent on the left and 42 per cent on the right.

Table 9.4 Attitudes to homosexual sex, among ideological groups on left-right scale, Scotland and England, 2000

column percentages	Scotland				England			
	left	centre	right	all	left	centre	right	all
always wrong	44	40	29	39	42	35	34	36
mostly wrong	7	9	10	9	11	9	10	10
sometimes wrong	5	7	14	8	5	9	10	9
rarely wrong	7	9	10	8	6	8	8	7
not wrong at all	32	28	33	29	33	35	34	34

Don't know and not answered included in base.

Percentages are weighted; for sample sizes, see Table 9.2.

source: Scottish Social Attitudes Survey 2000 and British Social Attitudes Survey 2000.

The Scottish government's position is perhaps more generally consistent with centre-ground opinion on the two other devolved matters we look at. The overwhelming majority of people in all ideological groups believe that it is definitely the government's responsibility to maintain the living standards of old people, as Table 9.5 shows. Indeed, in the centre and on the right, the support in Scotland for this is firmer than in England: 88 per cent as against 81 per cent in the centre, and 76 per cent against 71 per cent on the right. Although the question as asked in the survey was a general one, not relating specifically to the costs of long-term care, the pattern of views in the table suggests that any government action to help old people would be welcomed in Scotland, especially in the centre and on the left. That said, it must also be pointed out that the Scottish Labour Party are only reluctant converts to the idea that the state should pay for old people's long-term care.

Table 9.5 Attitude to responsibility for old people's standard of living, among ideological groups on left-right scale, Scotland and England, 2000

column percentages	Scotland				England			
	left	centre	right	all	left	centre	right	all
whether government's responsibility:								
definitely	90	88	76	85	89	81	71	80
probably	4	9	22	11	8	16	24	16
probably not	2	0	0.3	0.3	0	0.5	3	1
definitely not	0.4	0.3	1	0.5	1	0.3	1	0.5

Don't know and not answered included in base.

Percentages are weighted; for sample sizes, see Table 9.2.

source: Scottish Social Attitudes Survey 2000 and British Social Attitudes Survey 2000.

On teachers, Table 9.6 shows very firm support for the proposition that the daily management of schools ought to be in the hands of teachers and head teachers. People on the left and in the centre tend to be more favourable to teachers than to head teachers in this respect, and people on the right favour each group equally, but the very clear point from the table is that all ideological groups much prefer that educational professionals should be in charge of day-to-day operations, not pupils, not parents, not the local authority, not the Scottish government, and not the UK government. People do seem to be distinguishing between daily management and policy: questions in other surveys have shown that a very large majority believe that policy for education should be settled in the Scottish Parliament, not Westminster and not local councils (Paterson 2000a: 33). Since this approach is now the policy of the Scottish education minister – professional autonomy and Scottish policy making – Scottish Labour can be said to be in touch with majority opinion. But this, too, is a recent conversion: there was a widespread perception at least by teachers that Jack McConnell's Labour predecessors in the post of Scottish education minister were not supporters of professional autonomy (Paterson 2000b). So – as on state support for old people – the best that could be said is that Scottish Labour has caught up with popular opinion only in the last year or so. It has not been leading from the centre.

Table 9.6 View about who should be most responsible for the daily management of schools, among ideological groups on left-right scale, Scotland, 2000

column percentages	left	centre	right	all
Teachers in the school	35	33	30	32
Head-teacher	26	28	31	28
Pupils in the school	5	3	1	3
Parents of pupils in the school	14	12	12	13
Education Authority	11	11	12	12
Scottish Executive	8	8	11	9
UK government	1	2	3	2

Don't know and not answered included in base.

Percentages are weighted; for sample sizes, see Table 9.2.

source: Scottish Social Attitudes Survey 2000 and British Social Attitudes Survey 2000.

WHAT POLICIES DOES THE CENTRE SUPPORT? (II) RESERVED MATTERS

The first of the four reserved matters is on the general adequacy of the public financial support available to people who are unemployed. Does the sample think that benefits are too high and are a disincentive to seeking work? This is a Westminster matter because the social security system is reserved. The second question is a general one on whether taxes and public spending should rise, fall or be maintained at present levels. The third concerns whether government is responsible for ensuring full employment. These two are almost wholly Westminster matters since almost all taxation policy and most employment policy are reserved. The final question is on attitudes to the common European currency, a Westminster matter because foreign affairs are reserved. These four topics have been chosen because they represent some of the most important political issues that will, in due course, define the Blair government's reputation (apart from internal constitutional reform). The role of the state, the scope for increasing taxes to pay for public spending, and the relationship of the UK to Europe are central problems facing the left, they are topics on which they differ markedly from the Conservative opposition, and they are likely to dominate the second term of the UK New Labour government.

Table 9.7 Views about level of state benefits for unemployed people, among ideological groups on left-right scale, Scotland and England, 2000

column percentages	Scotland				England			
	left	centre	right	all	left	centre	right	all
Too low and cause hardship	54	44	30	43	51	42	25	40
Too high and discourage from finding jobs	24	28	32	28	31	36	48	37
Neither	12	16	21	17	13	15	15	15

Don't know and not answered included in base.

Percentages are weighted; for sample sizes, see Table 9.2.

source: Scottish Social Attitudes Survey 2000 and British Social Attitudes Survey 2000.

On the first of the four reserved matters – attitudes to the levels of benefits for people who are unemployed – Table 9.7 shows that opinion on the centre and on the left in Scotland is not sympathetic to the argument that they are so high that they are a disincentive to seeking work: only around a quarter take that view, in contrast to around a half believing that benefits are so low that they cause hardship. Only on the right is opinion more evenly balanced. In England, however, only the left resembles the views found on the Scottish centre-left. Between 1999 and 2000, the trend was for more people to favour the view that benefits are too low, and fewer to believe that they are too high. So the distinctive Scottish centre in

Table 9.7 is a phenomenon that has been emerging since the Scottish Parliament election, and the Scottish centre now has views on this matter that are as close to the English left as to the English centre.

On taxes and spending, there was little difference between Scotland and England, because opinion both on the left and in the centre in both countries favours higher taxes and spending: see Table 9.8. Only on the right is the modal position the same as the government's – that taxes and spending should be kept the same or reduced.

Table 9.8 Attitude to taxation and spending, among ideological groups on left-right scale, Scotland and England, 2000

column percentages	Scotland				England			
	left	centre	right	all	left	centre	right	all
Reduce taxes and spending	5	3	5	4	5	4	6	5
Keep taxes and spending the same	32	40	46	39	31	39	48	39
Raises taxes and spending	62	55	45	54	59	53	41	51

Don't know and not answered included in base.

Percentages are weighted; for sample sizes, see Table 9.2.

source: Scottish Social Attitudes Survey 2000 and British Social Attitudes Survey 2000.

These two questions thus place Scottish opinion, especially centre-ground opinion, firmly on the left on reserved matters, and to some extent to the left of opinion in England. The same was true of questions about other reserved areas of policy. For example, 49 per cent of Scots but only 39 per cent of the English believed that government is responsible for ensuring full employment. The difference was largest in the centre, where the level of agreement was 50 per cent in Scotland and 38 per cent in England. On the left, the proportions were 65 per cent and 56 per cent, and on the right they were 32 per cent and 26 per cent. Further confirmation that Scottish opinion is to the left of English opinion on reserved matters comes from the individual items that make up our scale, and which were shown in Table 9.1. These all relate primarily to reserved matters (since they relate to fiscal policy, social security policy, and employment policy). In each case, as Table 9.1 shows, overall Scottish opinion is at least slightly to the left of opinion in England. Further calculation showed that this is particularly so in the centre. For example, the proportions in the centre agreeing or agreeing strongly that government should redistribute wealth were 52 per cent in Scotland but only 36 per cent in England, a gap of sixteen points. On the left, the gap was just nine points (93 per cent and 84 per cent), and on the right the gap was also nine points (13 per cent and four per cent). Where it was possible to make a comparison with 1999 – that is, on redistribution, and on inequalities of wealth and of power – these differences between the Scottish and English centres were broadly stable over time.

On the euro, ideological position seems to make little difference to views in Scotland, whereas in England the right is more opposed. Thus in Scotland the opposition to the euro is 54 per cent on the left, 55 per cent in the centre and 51 per cent on the right. In England, the opposition is 61 per cent, 64 per cent and 72 per cent. When the eventual referendum comes, the government in England may find itself in a battle with the right which it will not face in Scotland. Again, these differences were similar to those of 1999.

WHAT ARE THE POLITICS OF THE CENTRE?

The last set of issues concerns the politics of the centre in Scotland. We look at two matters: attitudes to the constitution, and party support. We also look at two sociological features of the Scottish ideological groups – national identity and social class.

The Scottish centre is highly distinctive culturally compared to the centre in England, as Table 9.9 shows. All ideological groups in Scotland are predominantly Scottish in their allegiance, while in England Britishness is stronger. But the notable difference in Scotland is that the centre more resembles the left in this respect than it does the right, whereas in England the centre is closer to the right. Thus the proportions saying they are 'Scottish not British' or 'Scottish more than British' are 75 per cent on the left, 70 per cent in the centre, but only 56 per cent on the right. In England, the corresponding proportions are 36 per cent on the left, 32 per cent in the centre and 31 per cent on the right. Governing from the centre in England thus implies a fairly strong measure of Britishness. Governing from the centre in Scotland signifies Scottishness, and indeed attempting to govern with a British accent would tend to be interpreted as being associated with the right.

Table 9.9 National identity of ideological groups on left-right scale, Scotland and England, 2000

column percentages	Scotland				England			
	left	centre	right	all	left	centre	right	all
Scottish/English, not British	50	38	22	37	23	18	16	18
Scottish/English more than British	25	32	34	31	13	14	15	14
Equally Scottish/English and British	14	20	27	21	30	35	34	34
British more than Scottish/English	2	2	6	3	11	14	15	14
British, not Scottish/English	2	3	6	4	13	10	14	12

Don't know and not answered included in base.

Percentages are weighted; for sample sizes, see Table 9.2.

source: Scottish Social Attitudes Survey 2000 and British Social Attitudes Survey 2000.

Perhaps not surprisingly, then, the centre in Scotland is in favour of extending the Parliament's powers, as is the left: see Table 9.10. The total agreeing or strongly agreeing with this is 73 per cent on the left and 68 per cent in the centre. On the right, the proportion is just 52 per cent. What's more, support for extending powers rose more on the left and the centre than on the right between 1999 and 2000: up ten points on the left and the centre, but up five points on the right. Governing from this centre would require that the Scottish Labour Party take up a position that they are, at present, firmly against.

Table 9.10 View about powers of Scottish Parliament, among ideological groups on left-right scale, Scotland, 2000

column percentages	left	centre	right	all
The powers should be extended:				
strongly agree	36	22	13	23
agree	37	46	39	43
neither agree nor disagree	14	16	18	15
disagree	8	11	21	12
strongly disagree	4	4	8	5

Don't know and not answered included in base.

Percentages are weighted; for sample sizes, see Table 9.2.

source: Scottish Social Attitudes Survey 2000 and British Social Attitudes Survey 2000.

The final matter is party support. The survey question was not about voting in any particular election, but about the party which people feel closest to. On the face of it, Labour has no problems with its level of support, as Table 9.11 shows. In Scotland, as in England, it is the largest party both in the centre and on the left. However, there are two complications which make life awkward for Scottish Labour. In Scotland, the main rival in the centre is the SNP, as it is on the left. Only on the right is the main rival the Conservatives. In England, by contrast, the Conservatives are clearly the main rivals to Labour both in the centre and on the right. So being in the centre in Scotland requires Labour to pay attention to leftwards pressures, whereas being on the centre in England forces attention to the right. This point is accentuated if we look at changes in support between 1999 and 2000. In England, there were hardly any. In Scotland, however, Labour's support fell by sixteen points on the left (from 56 per cent to 40 per cent), and the SNP's rose by six points. In the centre, the SNP's support fell by six points, whereas Labour's fell by only three. No other changes were statistically significant.

Table 9.11 Party support of ideological groups on left-right scale, Scotland and England, 2000

column percentages	Scotland				England			
	left	centre	right	all	left	centre	right	all
Conservative	7	14	34	16	14	26	52	28
Labour	40	39	24	36	56	42	25	41
Liberal Democrat	5	8	10	8	11	12	8	11
SNP	27	20	14	20	-	-	-	-
Other party	2	2	0	2	1	0.4	0.5	1

Don't know and not answered included in base.

Percentages are weighted; for sample sizes, see Table 9.2.

source: Scottish Social Attitudes Survey 2000 and British Social Attitudes Survey 2000.

These changes are reflected also in the changing class composition of the Scottish ideological groups, unlike the stability in England. Social class strongly distinguished between the ideological groups, as Table 9.12 shows. In both countries, the left is predominantly working class, the right is even more strongly middle class, and the centre has fairly even representation from professional groups, non-professional white-collar occupations, and the working class. This feature of the centre is one of the things that captures the interest of New Labour, or indeed any centrist party: a party appealing to such a socially diverse group cannot easily be accused of being sectional. Nevertheless, a small but definite change took place in the class composition of the left-wing group in 2000 in Scotland. The proportion of it that was working class was up seven points on 1999 (from 36 per cent to 43 per cent), and the proportion that was in the salariat was down four points (23 per cent to 19 per cent). The salariat proportion in the right-wing group went in the other direction, from 43 per cent up to 50 per cent. No such changes took place in England.

**Table 9.12 Class composition of ideological groups on left-right scale,
Scotland and England, 2000**

column percentages	Scotland				England			
	left	centre	right	all	left	centre	right	all
Salariat	19	30	50	31	26	28	47	31
Petty bourgeoisie	9	7	8	8	5	6	9	7
Routine non-manual	18	21	22	21	16	26	23	23
Supervisors	10	9	4	8	9	9	5	8
Working class	43	33	16	32	43	30	14	29

Don't know and not answered included in base.

Percentages are weighted; for sample sizes, see Table 9.2.

source: *Scottish Social Attitudes Survey 2000 and British Social Attitudes Survey 2000.*

So it could be that, by attempting to govern from a common Britain-wide centre, Labour is alienating the Scottish left and pushing the working class to the left. Of course, it could well afford to do so, since it gets only one fifth of its vote from the left, and two thirds from the centre. The SNP, correspondingly, cannot afford to give up on the centre, since it gets 59 per cent of its vote there, and one quarter on the left. Neither party could afford to concentrate on the working class, from which they each get only one third of their vote (in line with that class's share of the total population: Table 9.12).

In that sense, both parties (and also the Liberal Democrats) are mainstream, since the ideological groups are represented among their support in broadly the same proportion as these groups constitute of the whole population. Only the Conservatives have skewed support, with 45 per cent of their support from the right and 47 per cent from the centre. The Tories in England are more mainstream, getting 54 per cent of their support from the centre and 37 per cent from the right. Labour's ideological support in England is much the same as in Scotland, even though the English centre is to the right of the Scottish centre: 25 per cent of their support comes from the left (compared to 21 per cent in Scotland) and 62 per cent from the centre (64 per cent in Scotland).

CONCLUSIONS

This analysis shows the complexities involved in claiming to govern from the centre where there are two centres, both of popular views and of legislative power. Scottish Labour seems sometimes not to know where to position itself. It is not very close to the centre on the highly complex matter of tuition fees, and indeed is possibly closer to the right than to any of the other two ideological groups (although not on the matter of how the proceeds of the new endowment contributions should be spent). It is definitely not in the centre on homosexuality. It has been dragged into the centre ground on state support for old people, and only the schools examinations crisis of summer 2000 brought an education minister that would respect the autonomy of teachers in the way that majority Scottish opinion does.

On some key policy matters that are reserved to Westminster, the Scottish centre is at best sceptical about Labour's approach. Except on the right, there is only minority and declining support for a view that the benefits system is a disincentive to unemployed people's seeking work. This was also true of attitudes to employment policy and to redistribution. In Scotland, the centre more closely resembles the left than the right in this respect, whereas in England the centre is rather closer to the right. In both Scotland and England, the centre supports raising taxes to pay for better public services, and it is the right which is closest to Labour's apparent position that taxes should not be increased. On the euro, the battle for Labour in England will be with a highly sceptical right, whereas in Scotland there is no such ideological polarisation.

More generally, part of the problem for Labour is that the Scottish centre is to the left of the centre in England. The party competition in Scotland – where the SNP, not the Conservative Party, is the main challenger to Labour – further encourages centre politics to look leftwards rather than to the right, especially in the context of a broadly proportional electoral system. And on its left, Labour sees an ideological group that is more working class than the cross-class coalition that Tony Blair has assembled with such electoral success in England. The Scottish centre resembles the left also in being firmly Scottish, and firmly in favour of extending the powers of the Scottish Parliament.

There is, of course, no reason at all why political parties ought to be close to the centre's views on anything. As we noted earlier, Margaret Thatcher wasn't when it came to the privatisation of nationalised industries, and yet managed to take opinion with her. She also was never close to the centre on taxes and public spending, and yet continued to win elections. That, it could be argued, is what political leadership is all about. The Scottish government – and indeed the Scottish political class generally – showed a very clear example of leadership over homosexuality, insisting that Section 2a be repealed even against popular opinion. Principled leadership of this type would have been much more acceptable to the Labour Party in the past than since the early 1990s. The reason that, despite this, it remains interesting to look at whether centre-ground views are close to those of the two governments is precisely this change in Labour's strategy: keeping close to the centre is how New Labour has presented itself. It has insisted that it governs from the centre, and it seems to have eschewed strong political leadership on controversial topics. The clearest example is on the euro, in stark contrast to the Scottish government's stance on Section 2a. The UK government has provided only weak leadership, postponing the decision for as long as it seems electorally expedient to do so.

Nevertheless, as the 2001 UK general election showed, the most impressive feature of Scottish Labour at the moment is its capacity to be ambiguous. It is both Scottish and British. It is both left-of-centre and centrist. It is both able to speak for Scottish centrist opinion (which tends to the left when compared to centrist opinion in England) and also be loyal to its colleagues in the south. It could be, indeed, that the very existence of two legislatures facilitates this useful ambiguity. Scottish Labour can present a somewhat left-wing and clearly Scottish face through the Holyrood Parliament, while also being part of the more centrist and more British majority in Westminster. Whether it can continue to be successful with this ambiguity remains to be seen, especially in the light of our findings here that it is on reserved matters that the Scottish centre is most to the left of the English centre. It may be that Scottish Labour will be forced by its own centrist logic to advocate some significant fiscal powers for the Scottish Parliament. If so, it will be able to lead from a position of strength. With the continuing decline of the Tories, the relative smallness of the Liberal Democrats, and the failure of the SNP to force Scottish politics to be dominated mainly by Scottish topics, Labour at present seems to be the only party that can embrace all this ambiguity about where the centre lies in Scotland with relative ease and with relative electoral popularity.

REFERENCES

Blair, T. (1998), *The Third Way*, London: Fabian Society.

Blair, T. (2001), Tony Blair's First Keynote Speech of the Campaign, Sedgefield, available at Labour Party web site: www.labour.org.uk.

Giddens, A. (1994), *Beyond Left and Right*, Cambridge: Polity.

Giddens, A. (1998), *The Third Way*, Cambridge: Polity.

Heath, A., Evans, G. and Martin, J. (1994), 'The measurement of core beliefs and values', *British Journal of Political Science*, 24, pp. 115-31.

Heath, A., Jowell, R. and Curtice, J. (2001), *The Rise of New Labour*, Oxford: Oxford University Press.

Paterson, L. (2000a), *Education and the Scottish Parliament*, Edinburgh: Dunedin Academic Press.

Paterson, L. (2000b), *Crisis in the Classroom: The Exam Debacle and the Way Ahead for Scottish Education*, Edinburgh: Mainstream.

Paterson, L., Brown, A., Curtice, J., Hinds, K., McCrone, D., Park, A., Sproston, K. and Surridge, P. (2001), *New Scotland, New Politics?*, Edinburgh: Edinburgh University Press.

10

CONCLUSIONS

We have now explored in some detail Scotland's social and political ties, the country's links with the rest of the UK and the links among and between its citizens. So what picture have we found? How strong or weak were Scots' ties with their political system in summer 2000, after the devolved Scottish Parliament had been in place for a year? And how strong or weak were some of the country's social institutions in the face of social change?

In many respects Scots' political ties with the rest of the United Kingdom were still strong. In summer 2000, independence attracted only minority support. The views of people in Scotland about most aspects of public policy continued to be similar to those of people in England. And, indeed, while they were far from sure that the situation was desirable, Scots also believed that the UK government, not the Scottish Parliament, had most influence over the way that Scotland is run.

But this does not mean that the setting up of the devolved parliament had necessarily encouraged Scots to feel closer to their political system. Rather, our findings suggest that, in its early days, devolution had had too little impact for that to be the case. In summer 2000, trust and confidence in politicians and the political system were both no higher in Scotland than they were in England, while they had also declined as much north of the border as they had in England between 1997 and 2000. Although Scots clearly did trust the Scottish Parliament to look after Scotland's interests more than they did the UK government, even here confidence had declined. Moreover there were signs that people had become more pessimistic, or perhaps realistic, about the capacity of a devolved parliament to achieve worthwhile social reform.

However, this does not mean that Scots did not want devolution to work. As we have already noted, in summer 2000 many Scots were clearly unhappy that Westminster still appeared to have so much influence north of the border and would have liked the Scottish Parliament to have had more powers. Indeed, the proportion thinking this increased over the first year of the parliament's life. And only one in eight Scots would have preferred that Scotland did not have its own parliament at all.

In reality, of course, devolution has indeed affected how Scotland is run. However, even where the Scottish Executive has been successfully putting in place policies that are distinctive from those in the rest of Britain – such as over student tuition fees, the financing of long-term personal care for older people, and a more liberal policy on homosexuality – this has not always meant that it has pursued policies that are more in tune with Scottish public opinion. On some matters the Executive is closer to Scottish opinion (as measured in summer 2000) than the UK government is to opinion in England – notably on care of old people and on giving teachers more say in the daily management of schools. But the Executive is further away from public opinion than is the UK government on student finance and on homosexuality. Evidently, devolved government is no neater than a unitary state.

If the long-term impact of devolution on Scots' attitudes towards their political system remains uncertain, the impact of recent social change on attitudes to those social institutions that shaped the ties that Scots have with each other is clear. Religion has traditionally played a key role in Scotland's life, and the views of the nation's religious leaders still receive widespread publicity in its press. But, in truth, there has been a sharp drop over the last two decades in religious observance, a drop which looks set to continue as more religious older generations are replaced by more secular younger ones. Scotland is still more religious than its English neighbour, but it appears that the gap has been closing fast.

Marriage too appears increasingly to be less important than it once was. While it is still seen to be an ideal, it is clear that cohabitation is now acceptable to a majority of Scots, while the minority who believe that sex before marriage is wrong has continued to diminish. Indeed, in summer 2000 there was considerable support for changing the law so that cohabitees could secure rights that are currently restricted to those who are married.

The result is a country that is gradually becoming more liberal in its social attitudes, a country in which such issues as sexuality and abortion are considered to be ones where individuals decide for themselves what is right and wrong rather than having to accept a moral code imposed on them by social institutions. Even when the potential consequences of some personal choices are thought to be undesirable, as in the case of teenage pregnancy, there is considerable support for more sex education and easier contraception rather than simply moral preaching. In the light of all this, there can be no doubt that the significance of the public debate about homosexuality in 1999-2000 was badly misinterpreted by many politicians and journalists. Rather than showing that Scotland is still a morally conservative country, it may well have been a sign of a nation coming to terms with an apparently more liberal future.

But if some of the country's social institutions are in decline and moral liberalism is on the rise, we might wonder what social ties are left to help bind the nation together. In fact there appear to be plenty. People are commonly still willing to trust each other, and, while they might consider it acceptable not to pay taxes that they ought to, they do not consider it fair to cheat on each other. A significant proportion are willing to join their fellow Scots in membership of social organisations. In other words, Scotland still appears to have a fair stock of social capital. Scots also share a common feeling of Scottish nationality, regardless of the region to which they belong. Although Scottish regionalism is strong it is not fissiparous.

We have found that moral liberalism and social capital tend to go together. Those who join organisations are also those who are most likely to adopt liberal positions on social issues. They are more likely as well to have faith in the principle of devolution within the United Kingdom, as opposed to independence. Altogether, much of our evidence supports the notion that a new devolved Scotland will be a liberal Scotland, much as many advocates of devolution hoped.

Even so, here too the success of the devolution project cannot be considered to be assured, in the sense that the possibility of a move towards a more powerful parliament has not been foreclosed. By summer 2000, the merely devolved parliament had not yet connected with those who are socially excluded – those who have little social capital, little education, and little prospect of high-status jobs. Such people are more sceptical of the UK state, tend to reject a British identity in favour of a Scottish one, are firmly on the left politically, and are not particularly liberal on moral issues. This is the social basis of Scottish nationalism and Scottish socialism, and its strength is the main reason we have for concluding that Scottish social ties are neither uniformly inclusive nor inevitably linked to a British future for the nation as a whole.

There have been limitations to the kinds of analysis that we have reported here. We have mainly reported Scots' own views of their various social ties, rather than an objective analysis of these ties. Even then, it is difficult in surveys fully to reflect the complex range of emotional attachments which people have to their families, their communities or the nations of Scotland and of Britain. Moreover, our data were collected just twelve months after the Scottish Parliament was set up, too soon to start casting definitive judgement on its success.

But there are also two key strengths to the analysis we have been able to pursue here. First, because our findings are based on the results of a large representative sample of people in Scotland, we can be sure that the picture that they paint is a fair reflection of what, in summer 2000, Scots thought about the questions that we were able to ask them. Second, while these may be early days for devolution, our survey enables us objectively and dispassionately to chart its progress from the beginning, thereby giving Scotland vital information on how well its politicians are doing and where they might need to improve. Our aim in the Scottish Social Attitudes project is to continue to monitor how Scotland does and does not change in the years ahead.

APPENDIX

TECHNICAL ASPECTS OF THE SURVEYS

Most data in the book are drawn from the 2000 Scottish Social Attitudes Survey. This was the second year of the study, which started in 1999 with the Scottish Parliamentary Election Survey (Paterson et al 2001). The series is parallel to the long-established British Social Attitudes Survey (Jowell et al 1999). Other surveys from which data have been used are the Scottish Election Surveys of 1979 1992 and 1997, and the 1997 Scottish Referendum Survey. Data from all the surveys are, or will be, publicly available through the Data Archive at the University of Essex.

DETAILS OF THE 2000 SCOTTISH SOCIAL ATTITUDES SURVEY

The study was funded by the Economic and Social Research Council (grant number R000238065). The survey involved a face-to-face interview with 1663 respondents and a self-completion questionnaire completed by 1505 of these people. Copies of the questionnaires are available from the National Centre for Social Research, web site www.natcen.ac.uk.

SAMPLE DESIGN

The Scottish Social Attitudes Survey was designed to yield a representative sample of adults aged 18 or over in Scotland. People were eligible for the survey if they were aged 18 when the interviewer first made contact with them. The sampling frame for the survey was the Postcode Address File (PAF), a list of addresses (or postal delivery points) compiled by the Post Office.

For practical reasons, the sample was confined to those living in private households. People living in institutions (such as nursing homes or hospitals – though not in private households at such institutions) were excluded, as were households whose addresses were not on the Postcode Address File. The sampling method involved a multi-stage design, with three separate stages of selection: selection of sectors, addresses and individuals:

1. At the first stage, postcode sectors were selected systematically from a list of all postal sectors in Scotland. Before selection, any sectors with fewer than 500 addresses were identified and grouped together with an adjacent sector. Sectors were then stratified on the basis of grouped council areas[1], population density (with variable banding used, in order to create three equal-sized strata per sub-region) and percentage of household heads recorded as employers/managers (from the 1991 Census). Ninety six postcode sectors were selected, with probability proportional to the number of addresses in each sector.

2. Thirty one addresses were selected at random in each of the 96 sectors. In some places more than one accommodation space shares an address. The Multiple Occupancy Indicator (MOI) on the Postcode Address File shows whether this is known to be the case. If the MOI indicated more than one accommodation space at a given address, the chances of the given address being selected from the list of addresses was increased to match the total number of accommodation spaces. As would be expected, the majority of MOIs had a value of one (92 per cent of those where an interview was obtained). The remainder, which ranged between three and 16, were incorporated into the weighting procedures (described below). In total the sample comprised 2976 addresses and each sample point issued to interviewers contained 31 addresses.

3. Interviewers called at each selected address, identified its eligibility, and, where an address was eligible, listed all residents eligible for inclusion in the sample – that is, all persons currently aged 18 or over residing at the selected address. The interviewer then selected one respondent using a computer-generated random selection procedure.

WEIGHTING

Data were weighted to take account of the fact that not all the units covered in the survey had the same probability of selection. The weighting reflected the relative selection probabilities of the individual at the three main stages of selection: address, household and individual.

First, because addresses were selected using the Multiple Output Indicator (MOI), weights had to be applied to compensate for the greater probability of an address with an MOI of more than one being selected, compared to an address with an MOI of one. Secondly, data were weighted to compensate for the fact that dwelling units at an address which contained a large number of dwelling units were less likely to be selected for inclusion in the survey than ones which did not share an address. (We used this procedure because in most cases these two stages will cancel each other out, resulting in more efficient weights.) Thirdly, data were weighted to compensate for the lower selection probabilities of adults living in large households compared with those living in small households. All weights fell within a range between 0.0359 and 4.5942. The weighted sample was scaled down to make the number of weighted productive cases exactly equal to the number of unweighted productive cases.

All the percentages presented in this book are based on weighted data; unweighted samples sizes are shown in the tables.

FIELDWORK

Interviewing was carried out between June and October 2000 (87 per cent of interviews being completed by the end of August). An advance letter telling people living at selected addresses that an interviewer would call was sent out before the interviewers called.

Fieldwork was conducted by interviewers drawn from the National Centre's regular panel and conducted using face-to-face computer-assisted interviewing. (Computer assisted interviewing involves the use of laptop computers during the interview, with questions appearing on the computer screen and interviewers entering responses directly into the computer.) Interviewers attended a one-day briefing conference to familiarise them with the questionnaires and procedures for selecting addresses and individuals to interview.

The average interview length was 48 minutes. Interviewers achieved an overall response rate of 65 per cent. Details are shown in Table A.1.

All respondents were asked to fill in a self-completion questionnaire which, whenever possible, was collected by the interviewer, but in some cases was posted to the National Centre. Up to three postal reminders were sent to obtain the maximum number of self-completion supplements.

A total of 157 respondents (9 per cent of those interviewed) did not return their self-completion questionnaire. We judged that it was not necessary to apply additional weights to correct for this non-response.

Table A.1: Response rates

	Number	%
Addresses issued	2976	
Vacant, derelict and other out of scope[1]	409	13.7
In scope	2567	100.0
Interview achieved	1663	64.8
Interview not achieved	904	35.2
Refused[2]	600	23.3
Non-contacted[3]	121	4.7
Other non-response	120	4.7

[1] *'Deadwood' included 31 addresses found to be in England as well as empty or holiday homes and businesses or institutions.*

[2] *'Refusals' comprise refusals before selection of an individual at the address, refusals to the office, refusal by the selected person, 'proxy' refusals (on behalf of the selected respondent) and broken appointments after which the selected person could not be re-contacted.*

[3] *'Non-contacts' comprise households where no one was contacted and those where the selected person could not be contacted.*

OTHER SURVEYS USED IN THE BOOK

SCOTTISH ELECTION SURVEYS

The Scottish Parliamentary Election Survey was carried out in 1999, and full details of its sample design etc – which were very similar to those described above for the 2000 survey – are given by Paterson et al (2001). It, too, was funded by the Economic and Social Research Council (ESRC). Scottish Election Surveys have been carried out as part of a series of British Election Surveys undertaken in 1974, 1979, 1992 and 1997. The British Election Surveys, which have been conducted since 1964, take place immediately after each general election. Since the 1970s, the ESRC has been involved in funding each of these surveys (other funders for some surveys have included the Gatsby Foundation – one of the Sainsbury family charitable trusts – and Pergamon Press). The surveys have been directed by various people and organisations over the years.

In this book we use data from the 1979, 1992 and 1997 Scottish Election Surveys. Fieldwork and data preparation for the 1992 and 1997 surveys were carried out by the National Centre for Social Research (then called Social and Community Planning Research). The Scottish samples were boosted in each of these years to allow data to be analysed for Scotland independently of Britain. The samples for each study were chosen using random selection modified by stratification and clustering. Up to 1992, the sampling frame was the electoral register (ER); in 1997 it was the Postcode Address File (PAF). Weights can be applied to make the 1997 survey (PAF) comparable with the previous (ER) samples.

Achieved sample sizes for Scotland were:

1979   729   (response rate 61 per cent)

1992   957   (response rate 74 per cent)

1997   882   (response rate 62 per cent)

Weighting of the data was carried out in each year to take account of unequal selection probabilities. The surveys involved self-completion supplements in 1992 and 1997, while in 1979 face-to-face interviews were carried out in people's homes, supplemented by a self-completion questionnaire returned after the interview.

SCOTTISH REFERENDUM SURVEY

The Scottish Referendum Survey (alongside a comparative Welsh Referendum Survey) was undertaken in September-October 1997, funded by the ESRC (grant no. M5443/285/001). Fieldwork was carried out by the National Centre for Social Research and interviewing began immediately after the referendum.

The sample was designed to be representative of the adult population who were living in private households in Scotland and eligible to vote in the referendum. It was drawn from the PAF and involved stratification and clustering. Weighting of the data was subsequently carried out to correct for variable selection probabilities.

The survey involved a face-to-face interview, administered using a traditional paper questionnaire, and a self-completion questionnaire. The number of interviews carried out was 676, a response rate of 68 per cent. Self-completion questionnaires were obtained from 657 respondents (97 per cent of those interviewed).

BRITISH SOCIAL ATTITUDES SURVEY

The BSAS has been running annually since 1983. It aims to yield a representative sample of adults aged 18 and over living in Britain. Since 1993, the sampling frame has been the Postcode Address File. The sample is selected by methods similar to those used in the election surveys. The sample size has generally been between 3000 and 3500, of whom about 300-350 are in Scotland. The purpose of the surveys is to go beyond the work of opinion polls to collect information about underlying changes in people's attitudes and values. Further information on the BSAS is contained in each of the annual reports on it: for example, Jowell et al (1999).

CLASSIFICATIONS USED IN ANALYSIS

SOCIAL CLASS/SOCIO-ECONOMIC GROUP

Social class classifications are derived from people's occupations. Respondents in the Scottish Social Attitudes Survey were classified according to either their own occupation or that of their spouse/partner. Spouse/partner's job details were collected if the respondent was not economically active or retired. Otherwise, the respondent's job details were collected (unless never worked). In this book, occupations are categorised according to the Goldthorpe schema. This classifies occupations by their 'general comparability', considering such factors as sources and levels of income, economic security, promotion prospects, and level of job autonomy and authority. The Goldthorpe schema was derived from the OPCS Standard Occupational Classification (SOC) combined with employment status. Two versions of the schema are coded: the full schema has 11 categories; the 'compressed schema' combines these into the five classes shown below:

Salariat (professional and managerial)
Routine non-manual workers (office and sales)
Petty bourgeoisie (the self-employed, including farmers, with and without employees)
Manual foremen and supervisors
Working class (skilled, semi-skilled and unskilled manual workers, personal service and agricultural workers)

There is a residual category comprising those who have never had a job or who gave insufficient information for classification purposes.

PARTY IDENTIFICATION

Respondents were classified as identifying with a particular political party if they considered themselves supporters of that party, or as closer to it than to others, or more likely to support a party in the event of a general election.

NATIONAL IDENTITY

The survey uses a scale, known as the Moreno scale, to measure how people relate being Scottish and being British, if at all. Single identities, either Scottish or British, form the ends of the scale and these identities are equal at the mid-point. At points 2 and 4, one or other is stressed but both are included. The question asks:

Which, if any, of the following best describes how you see yourself?

Scottish, not British
More Scottish than British
Equally Scottish and British
More British than Scottish
British, not Scottish
None of these

A second survey measure also used is a simpler question that asks respondents to select one identity from a list. They are asked:

If you had to choose, which one best describes the way you think of yourself?

British, English, European, Irish, Northern Irish, Scottish, Welsh, None of these

ATTITUDE SCALES

The Scottish Social Attitudes Survey included two attitude scales relating to political ideology. These were developed to measure where respondents stand on certain underlying value dimensions (Heath et al 1994). They are a left-right (socialist-laissez faire) scale and a liberal-authoritarian scale. Versions of the attitudes scales have been used since the 1986 BSAS and 1987 BES. Each scale consists of an aggregation of individual survey items designed to measure different aspects of the underlying belief system. A useful way of summarising the information from a number of questions of this sort is to construct an additive index (DeVellis 1991; Spector 1992). This approach rests on the assumption that there is an underlying – 'latent' – attitudinal dimension which characterises the answers to all the questions within each scale. If so, scores on the index are likely to be a more reliable indication of the underlying attitude than the answers to any one question.

The items are:

Left-right scale/Socialist – Laissez-faire scale

Government should redistribute income from the better off to those who are less well off.

Big business benefits owners at the expense of workers.

Ordinary working people do not get their fair share of the nation's wealth.

There is one law for the rich and one for the poor.

Management will always try to get the better of employees if it gets the chance.

Libertarian-authoritarian scale

Young people today don't have enough respect for Britain's traditional values.

People who break the law should be given stiffer sentences.

For some crimes, the death penalty is the most appropriate sentence.

Schools should teach children to obey authority.

The law should always be obeyed, even if a particular law is wrong.

Censorship of films and magazines is necessary to uphold moral standards.

Low values on the scales represent the socialist and liberal positions respectively. The scales have been tested for reliability (as measured by Cronbach's alpha). Values of 0.87 were obtained for the left-right scale and 0.85 for the libertarian-authoritarian scale in 2000. These levels of reliability can be considered 'very good' (DeVellis 1991).

There is also a scale measuring the respondents' sense of political efficacy. It is calculated from respondents' views on four statements about the political system:

Generally speaking, those we elect as MPs lose touch with people pretty quickly.

Parties are only interested in people's votes, not in their opinions.

It doesn't really matter which party is in power, in the end things go on much the same.

MPs don't care much about what people like me think.

Low values on this scale indicate high levels of cynicism about politicians, which can be thought of also as low levels of 'efficacy' – a weak sense that taking part in politics is worthwhile. The reliability here was 0.79, also very high.

DATA INTERPRETATION

STATISTICAL SIGNIFICANCE

All the data in the book come from samples of the population, meaning that they are subject to sampling error. However, it is possible to calculate confidence intervals relating to any value from a given sample, creating a range within which we can have a certain level of confidence that the true population value lies. Table A.2 gives an indication of the confidence intervals that apply to different percentage results for different sample sizes. Ninety-five per cent confidence intervals are shown, meaning that we can be 95 per cent sure that the true answer lies within the range shown. For example, for a percentage result of 50 per cent based on a sample of 500 there is a 95 per cent chance that the true result lies within +/- 4 per cent (thus, between 46 per cent and 54 per cent).

These confidence limits assume a simple random sample with no adjustment made for the effects of clustering the sample into a number of sample points. Although such an adjustment would increase the confidence limits slightly, in most cases these would not differ notably from those shown on the table (Paterson 2000: Appendix). It should be noted that certain types of variables (those most associated with the area a person lives in) are more affected by clustering than others. For example, Labour identifiers and local authority tenants tend to be concentrated in certain areas and so, were the effect of the sample's being clustered taken into account, the confidence intervals around such variables would widen more than would be the case for many attitudinal variables (Jowell et al 1999).

Table A.2 Confidence intervals for survey findings

Sample size	Approximate 95 per cent confidence limits for a percentage result of:		
	10 per cent or 90 per cent +/-	30 per cent or 70 per cent +/-	50 per cent +/-
50	8	13	14
100	6	9	10
250	4	6	6
500	3	4	4
1,000	2	3	3
2,000	1	2	2

Tests of statistical significance take account of the confidence intervals attached to survey findings. They can be carried out using modelling techniques (such as those described below), or by hand. Whenever comments on differences between sub-groups of the sample are made in this book, these differences have been tested and found to be statistically significant at the 95 per cent level or above. Similarly, although standard deviations are mostly not presented alongside mean figures in this book, these have been calculated and used to verify the statistical significance of the differences between mean figures which are commented on.

STATISTICAL MODELLING

For many of the more complex analyses in the book, we have used logistic or linear regression models to assess whether there is reliable evidence that particular variables are associated with each other.

Regression analysis aims to summarise the relationship between a 'dependent' variable and one or more 'independent' explanatory variables. It shows how well we can estimate a respondent's score on the dependent variable from knowledge of their scores on the independent variables. The technique takes into account relationships between the different independent variables (for example, between education and income, or social class and housing tenure). Linear regression is often undertaken to support a claim that the phenomena measured by the independent variables cause the phenomenon measured by the dependent variable. However, the causal ordering, if any, between the variables cannot be verified or falsified by the technique. Causality can only be inferred through special experimental designs or through assumptions made by the analyst. Logistic regression is, in its logical structure, the same as linear regression, but it is used to model variables which are dichotomous – for example, voting or not voting.

An example of linear regression can be found in Chapter 3, where the technique is used to investigate factors which are associated with attitudes towards marriage. Several factors which might explain these attitudes are included in the model (age, level of education, sex, religion and religious attendance, social class, political party identification, newspaper readership, main source of income, housing tenure, marital status, and whether the respondent had a child while they were a teenager or later). Although simple cross-tabulations may suggest that all of these characteristics are associated with turnout, because many are themselves associated with one another it is not possible to assess whether their association with turnout is 'real' or spurious. In this case – as discussed in Chapter 3 – the model identifies only some of these factors as having an independent significant effect on turnout.

Full technical details of regression can be found in many textbooks on social statistics, for example Bryman and Cramer (1997).

FACTOR ANALYSIS

Factor analysis is a statistical technique which aims to identify whether there are one or more apparent sources of commonality to the answers given by respondents to a set of questions. It ascertains the smallest number of factors (or dimensions) which can most economically summarise all of the variation found in the set of questions being analysed. Factors are established where respondents who give a particular answer to one question in the set tend to give the same answer as each other to one or more of the other questions in the set. The technique is most useful when a relatively small number of factors is able to account for a relatively large proportion of the relationships among all of the questions in the set.

The technique produces a factor loading for each question (or variable) on each factor. Where questions have a high loading on the same factor then it will be the case that respondents who give a particular answer to one of these questions tend to give a similar answer to the other questions. Examples of the use of factor analysis are found in Chapter 3.

REFERENCES

Bryman, A. and Cramer, D. (1997), *Quantitative Data Analysis*, London: Routledge.

DeVellis, R. F (1991), *Scale Development: Theory and Applications*, Newbury Park, Ca.: Sage.

Heath, A., Evans, G., and Martin, J. (1994), 'The measurement of core beliefs and values', *British Journal of Political Science*, 24, pp. 115-31.

Jowell, R., Curtice, J., Park, A. and Thomson, K. (eds) (1999), *British Social Attitudes: the 16th Report.*, Aldershot: Ashgate.

Paterson, L. (2000), 'The social class of Catholics in Scotland', Statistics in Society, *Journal of the Royal Statistical Society* (Series A), 163, pp. 363-79.

Paterson, L., Brown, A., Curtice, J., Hinds, K., McCrone, D., Park, A., Sproston, K. and Surridge, P. (2001), *New Scotland, New Politics?*, Edinburgh: Edinburgh University Press.

Spector, P. E. (1992), *Summated Rating Scale Construction: an Introduction*, Newbury Park, Ca.: Sage.

---

[1] Group 1: Scottish Borders; Dumfries & Galloway; South Ayrshire; East Ayrshire, South Lanarkshire; North Ayrshire.

Group 2: Inverclyde; West Dunbartonshire; Renfrewshire; East Renfrewshire; Glasgow City; East Dunbartonshire.

Group 3: North Lanarkshire; Falkirk; West Lothian; Edinburgh; Midlothian; East Lothian.

Group 4: Argyll and Bute; Stirling; Perth and Kinross; Clackmannanshire; Fife; Angus; Dundee.

Group 5: Comhairle nan Eilean Siar; Orkney; Shetland; Highland; Moray; Aberdeenshire; Aberdeen.